Weight Watchers

Cook It Quick!

SPEEDY LOW-*POINT* RECIPES IN 30 MINUTES OR LESS

A Word About Weight Watchers

Since 1963, Weight Watchers has grown from a handful of people to millions of members annually. Today, Weight Watchers is recognized as one of the leading names in safe and sensible weight control. Weight Watchers members form a diverse group, from youths to senior citizens, attending meetings around the globe.

Although weight-loss and weight-management results vary by individual, we recommend that you attend Weight Watchers meetings, follow the Weight Watchers food plan, and participate in regular physical activity. For the Weight Watchers meeting nearest you, call (800) 651-6000. Visit our Web site at WeightWatchers.com.

Weight Watchers Publishing Group
Creative and Editorial Director: Nancy Gagliardi
Production Manager: Alan Biederman
Office Manager/Publishing Assistant: Jenny Laboy-Brace

Editor: Barbara Turvett
Art Director: Ed Melnitsky
Photography: Elizabeth Watt, Ann Stratton
Food Styling: Paul Grimes, Rori Spinelli

Printed in the USA.

RECIPE SYMBOLS

 hot/fiery

 one pot

 no cooking

 vegetarian

contents

salads to sink your teeth into

Crab Salad in Cantaloupe

Crab Salad in Cantaloupe

 MAKES 4 SERVINGS

Although this salad has a somewhat retro, bridge-club-luncheon feel, it's much lighter than its fifties' predecessors. But that doesn't stop it from being oh so filling!

¼ **cup + 2 tablespoons plain**
 fat-free yogurt
2 **tablespoons reduced-calorie**
 mayonnaise
1 **tablespoon chopped parsley**
1 **tablespoon chopped tarragon**
1 **scallion, sliced**
1 **tablespoon tarragon vinegar**
½ **pound crabmeat or surimi, picked**
 over and flaked
1 **celery stalk, thinly sliced**
2 **small cantaloupes, halved and seeded**
½ **bunch watercress, stemmed**
 (about 2 cups)
4 **cherry tomatoes, halved**

1. Puree the yogurt, mayonnaise, parsley, tarragon, scallion, and vinegar in a food processor or blender.
2. Combine the crabmeat and celery in a bowl. Pour in the dressing; toss to coat. Scoop the salad into the cantaloupe halves. Line 4 plates with the watercress and place the cantaloupe on top. Garnish with the cherry tomatoes.

Per serving: 176 Cal, 4 g Fat, 1 g Sat Fat, 60 mg Chol, 256 mg Sod, 22 g Carb, 3 g Fib, 15 g Prot, 158 mg Calc. *POINTS: 3.*

cooking flash

To prevent the cantaloupe halves from rolling around, slice a thin piece of rind off the bottom of each. If you like, scoop some of the cantaloupe into balls and add them to the crab salad. You may also want to line the cantaloupe halves with watercress before adding the salad.

Warm Lentil Salad

MAKES 4 SERVINGS

Because lentils are said to bring financial luck, they are traditionally served in Italy on New Year's Day to ensure riches in the coming year.

1 **cup lentils, picked over, rinsed, and drained**
2 **garlic cloves, bruised and peeled**
1 **bay leaf**
6 **cups water**
1 **carrot, thinly sliced**
3 **celery stalks, thinly sliced**
1 **onion, chopped**
½ **cup diced seeded green bell pepper**
¼ **cup finely chopped mint**
¼ **cup finely chopped parsley**
¼ **cup dry white wine**
4 **teaspoons extra-virgin olive oil**
4 **teaspoons white-wine vinegar**
¼ **teaspoon salt**
Freshly ground pepper, to taste

1. Bring the lentils, garlic, bay leaf, and water to a boil. Reduce the heat, cover, and simmer until the lentils are barely tender, about 15 minutes. Drain the lentils, discarding the garlic and bay leaf.
2. Combine the carrot, celery, onion, bell pepper, mint, parsley, wine, oil, vinegar, salt, and ground pepper in a bowl. Stir in the lentils. Cover and let stand until slightly warm; do not refrigerate.

Per serving: 224 Cal, 5 g Fat, 1 g Sat Fat, 0 mg Chol, 171 mg Sod, 31 g Carb, 7 g Fib, 13 g Prot, 56 mg Calc. *POINTS: 4.*

cooking flash

Bruising garlic releases its flavor. To bruise the garlic, press it with the flat side of a knife just hard enough to flatten it slightly.

Tijuana Salad

MAKES 4 SERVINGS

This is sure to become a speedy favorite. Serve the filling salad with warmed tortillas on the side. We like this with mild salsa, but use whatever heat level you prefer.

1 (16-ounce) can black beans, rinsed and drained
1 (16-ounce) can pink beans, rinsed and drained
1 (11-ounce) jar salsa
1 teaspoon ground cumin
4 cups mixed baby greens
½ cup shredded reduced-fat taco cheese blend
½ cup plain fat-free yogurt

1. In a nonstick saucepan, heat the black beans, pink beans, salsa, and cumin to serving temperature.
2. Divide the greens among 4 salad plates. Spoon ½ cup of the bean mixture over each serving of greens and sprinkle with the cheese, then dollop each with 2 tablespoons of yogurt.

Per serving: 271 Cal, 5 g Fat, 2 g Sat Fat, 8 mg Chol, 1,143 mg Sod, 41 g Carb, 14 g Fib, 19 g Prot, 308 mg Calc. *POINTS: 5.*

Speedy Salad Strategies

To save time during the week, set up a salad bar in your refrigerator on the weekend. In separate containers, refrigerate:

- washed romaine lettuce wrapped in paper towels
- blanched broccoli and green bell peppers
- cleaned, cut-up carrots, red bell peppers, cucumbers, and fennel
- prepared whole grains (like bulghur), rice, and pasta shapes

Also, keep on hand cans of beans, sliced beets, and fruit packed in its own juice.

Grilled Chicken and Bean Salad

MAKES 4 SERVINGS

This versatile salad can be served as a first course for dinner or as a luncheon entrée. It is as delicious warm as it is at room temperature.

¼ **cup fresh lemon juice**
3 **teaspoons chopped rosemary**
3 **garlic cloves, peeled**
1 **pound skinless boneless chicken breasts**
1 **(19-ounce) can cannellini beans, rinsed and drained**
1 **tomato, peeled, seeded, and finely chopped**
¼ **teaspoon salt**
⅛ **teaspoon freshly ground pepper**

1. Combine the lemon juice and 1 teaspoon of the rosemary in a bowl, then press in 1 garlic clove with a garlic press. Add the chicken and let stand at room temperature about 15 minutes. Preheat the broiler.

2. Meanwhile, combine the beans, tomato, and the remaining 2 teaspoons of rosemary in a nonstick skillet. Press in the remaining 2 garlic cloves. Cook, stirring occasionally, 10 minutes. Stir in the salt and pepper.

3. Put the chicken on a broiler rack and broil until cooked through, about 5 minutes on each side. Thinly slice the chicken crosswise. Divide the bean mixture among 4 salad plates and top with the equally divided portions of chicken.

Per serving: 244 Cal, 2 g Fat, 0 g Sat Fat, 66 mg Chol, 502 mg Sod, 22 g Carb, 6 g Fib, 32 g Prot, 67 mg Calc. *POINTS: 4.*

Tex-Mex Chicken, Corn, and Black Bean Salad

 MAKES 4 SERVINGS

Combine Southwestern staples—corn, black beans, and salsa—with chicken and fresh veggies, and you'll have a robust main-dish salad everyone will love.

½ **pound cooked chicken breast, cut into thin strips**
1 **cup canned black beans, rinsed and drained**
1 **(10-ounce) box frozen corn kernels, thawed**
1 **tomato, coarsely chopped**
1 **red onion, thinly sliced**
1 **(11-ounce) jar salsa**
⅓ **cup red-wine vinegar**
2 **tablespoons chopped cilantro**
8 **large lettuce leaves**
12 **baked tortilla chips, crumbled**

1. Combine the chicken, beans, corn, tomato, onion, salsa, vinegar, and cilantro. Let stand at least 15 minutes.
2. Put 2 lettuce leaves on each of 4 plates. Divide the chicken mixture among the plates, then sprinkle with the tortilla chips.

Per serving: 321 Cal, 4 g Fat, 1 g Sat Fat, 48 mg Chol, 707 mg Sod, 46 g Carb, 6 g Fib, 27 g Prot, 67 mg Calc. **POINTS: 6.**

shopping flash

We like this with white corn tortilla chips, but try them with your favorite variety, or whatever is available in your supermarket.

Chicken Salad with Asian Flavors

MAKES 4 SERVINGS

The soft texture and flowery scent of lychees are a treat indeed. Look for them in cans year-round. If you happen to live near a city that has a large Asian population, you might be lucky enough to find fresh lychees in the spring and early summer in an Asian grocery or outdoor market.

2 tablespoons orange juice
1 tablespoon reduced-sodium soy sauce
1 tablespoon rice vinegar
2 teaspoons peanut oil
1 teaspoon sugar
1 teaspoon Dijon mustard
1½ cups shredded cooked skinless chicken breast
10 canned lychees in syrup, rinsed and drained
12 sweet cherries, pitted and halved
½ mango, cut into ½-inch cubes
1 carrot, shredded
2 celery stalks, diced
2 scallions, thinly sliced

1. Whisk the orange juice, soy sauce, vinegar, oil, sugar, and mustard in a small bowl until well blended.

2. Combine the chicken, lychees, cherries, mango, carrot, celery, and scallions in a salad bowl. Add the dressing; toss to combine.

Per serving: 159 Cal, 4 g Fat, 1 g Sat Fat, 36 mg Chol, 235 mg Sod, 16 g Carb, 2 g Fib, 14 g Prot, 29 mg Calc. *POINTS: 3.*

Fruited Turkey Salad

MAKES 4 SERVINGS

This is a refreshing and satisfying main-dish salad, and it's wonderfully versatile. Vary the fruit by what looks best at the market, or use dried fruit. White tuna would be a good substitute for the turkey. If your herb garden is in bloom, mix in a little dill, tarragon, or thyme.

¼ **cup plain low-fat yogurt**
3 **tablespoons reduced-calorie mayonnaise**
3 **scallions, thinly sliced**
1 **tablespoon cider vinegar**
¼ **teaspoon salt**
¼ **teaspoon freshly ground pepper**
1 **large apple, cored and finely diced**
1 **pear, cored and finely diced**
2 **cups cubed cooked turkey or chicken breast**
2 **carrots, shredded**
2 **celery stalks, thinly sliced**
8 **cups salad greens**

Whisk together the yogurt, mayonnaise, scallions, vinegar, salt, and pepper in a large bowl. Add the apple and pear; toss to coat. Add the turkey, carrots, and celery; toss again. Place the greens on a platter or 4 plates, then top with the turkey salad.

Per serving: 249 Cal, 6 g Fat, 1 g Sat Fat, 63 mg Chol, 330 mg Sod, 26 g Carb, 6 g Fib, 25 g Prot, 131 mg Calc. *POINTS: 5.*

cooking flash

You'll get the best results with turkey that isn't overcooked. If you don't have leftovers, poaching is an easy and gentle cooking method: Bring 2 inches of water to simmer in a deep skillet. Add 1 pound of skinless boneless turkey or chicken breast in a single layer. Reduce the heat and cook, covered, over very low heat until it is cooked through, about 30 minutes. Remove and let cool; refrigerate the poaching liquid and use in a recipe that calls for chicken broth.

Steak-and-Potato Salad

MAKES 4 SERVINGS

This salad is hearty enough to be filling, yet light enough to enjoy in the heat of the summer.

2 tablespoons red-wine vinegar
1 tablespoon extra-virgin olive oil
2 teaspoons minced fresh rosemary
½ teaspoon freshly ground pepper
½ teaspoon salt
2 tomatoes, diced
1 pound new potatoes, cooked
  and halved
2 cups thinly sliced cooked lean
  flank steak
2 cups sliced mushrooms
4 cups torn cleaned arugula or
  spinach leaves

1. Whisk the vinegar, oil, rosemary, pepper, and salt in a large bowl. Add the tomatoes; toss to coat. Let stand at least 20 minutes.

2. Add the potatoes, steak, and mushrooms to the tomatoes; toss to combine. Put 1 cup of the arugula on each of 4 plates; top with the salad.

Per serving: 254 Cal, 8 g Fat, 2 g Sat Fat, 28 mg Chol, 373 mg Sod, 30 g Carb, 5 g Fib, 16 g Prot, 78 mg Calc. *POINTS: 5*.

cooking flash

Flank steak is thin and fibrous, but very flavorful. Marinate it briefly before cooking to help tenderize it, and slice it against the grain.

Beef Fajita Salad

MAKES 4 SERVINGS

Beer is the secret ingredient in the marinade; it adds a subtle flavor. Liquid smoke is available in mesquite as well as hickory flavor; look for it in the spice section of your supermarket. For an even prettier salad, use any combination of red, green, yellow, or orange bell peppers.

1 (12-ounce) bottle beer
¼ cup chopped cilantro
3 scallions, sliced
1 tablespoon Worcestershire sauce
2 garlic cloves, smashed
½ teaspoon salt
¼ teaspoon cayenne
2 teaspoons hickory-flavored liquid smoke
¾ pound skirt steak, trimmed of all visible fat
2 bell peppers, halved, seeded, and deveined
1 large Vidalia onion, peeled and cut into wedges
1 large tomato, cored and cut into wedges
½ pound mixed salad greens
¼ cup light corn syrup

1. Whisk the beer, cilantro, scallions, Worcestershire sauce, garlic, salt, and cayenne in a large bowl; reserve ½ cup for the dressing. Stir the liquid smoke into the bowl, then add the steak, bell peppers, onion, and tomato; toss to coat. Let stand at room temperature 15 minutes.

2. Preheat the broiler. Place the steak and vegetables on the broiler rack; discard the marinade. Broil 3 inches from the heat until the vegetables are lightly browned and the meat is done to taste, about 5 minutes on each side for medium; turn the vegetables with the meat. Thinly slice the steak, peppers, and onions.

3. Divide the greens among 4 plates; top with the steak and vegetables. Whisk the corn syrup into the reserved beer mixture; drizzle the dressing over the salads.

Per serving: 254 Cal, 4 g Fat, 1 g Sat Fat, 53 mg Chol, 423 mg Sod, 29 g Carb, 3 g Fib, 22 g Prot, 65 mg Calc. *POINTS: 5.*

Duck, Pear, and Watercress Salad

MAKES 4 SERVINGS

Duck meat has a rich flavor and texture that's a perfect foil for pear, but you can use dark turkey meat if you prefer.

⅓ cup pear nectar
2 tablespoons hoisin sauce
2 tablespoons rice vinegar
4 teaspoons Asian (dark) sesame oil
1 tablespoon reduced-sodium soy sauce
1 teaspoon fresh lemon juice
¼ teaspoon cinnamon
⅛ teaspoon ground anise
1 (¾-pound) duck breast, skinned
3 pears, peeled, cored, and diced
½ bunch watercress, tough stems removed (about 2 cups)
1 (8-ounce) can sliced water chestnuts, drained
1 nectarine, sliced (optional)

1. Preheat the broiler. Spray the broiler rack with nonstick spray.
2. Whisk the pear nectar, hoisin sauce, vinegar, oil, soy sauce, lemon juice, cinnamon, and anise in a bowl. Place the duck on the broiler rack and brush with 2 tablespoons of the dressing. Broil 6 inches from the heat until cooked through, about 7 minutes on each side. Transfer to a cutting board and let cool slightly, then slice it thinly against the grain.
3. Add the pears, watercress, and water chestnuts to the remaining dressing; toss to coat. Divide the salad among 4 plates; top with the duck. Garnish with the nectarine slices, if desired.

Per serving: 245 Cal, 9 g Fat, 2 g Sat Fat, 66 mg Chol, 319 mg Sod, 24 g Carb, 7 g Fib, 18 g Prot, 15 mg Calc. *POINTS: 5.*

shopping flash

Most butchers and better supermarkets stock duck breast year-round. Purchase Muscovy duck if you find it, since it is leaner than other breeds.

Duck, Pear, and Watercress Salad

Tostada Salad

MAKES 4 SERVINGS

If you're a fan of the taco salad that many restaurants serve in the crispy tortilla bowl, try this tasty yet light version. It's packed with flavor and contrasting textures.

1 teaspoon vegetable oil
2 onions, diced
¼ pound lean ground beef
   (10% or less fat)
2 tablespoons chili powder
1 (14½-ounce) can Mexican-style
   diced tomatoes
½ teaspoon salt
4 cups shredded iceberg lettuce
3 tomatoes, chopped
¾ cup canned black beans,
   rinsed and drained
2 medium all-purpose potatoes,
   cooked and diced
½ medium avocado, peeled and diced
2 tablespoons red-wine vinegar
16 baked tortilla chips

1. Heat the oil in a nonstick skillet, then add about half of the onions. Sauté until softened, then add the ground beef. Brown the beef, breaking it apart with a spoon. Add the chili powder and stir to coat the beef thoroughly. Stir in the canned tomatoes and salt and cook, stirring frequently, until the mixture has thickened, about 10 minutes.

2. Combine the lettuce, chopped tomatoes, beans, potatoes, avocado, and the remaining onions in a salad bowl. Sprinkle with the vinegar; toss to combine.

3. Divide the tortilla chips among 4 plates; top with the vegetables, then with the beef mixture. Serve immediately.

Per serving: 453 Cal, 12 g Fat, 2 g Sat Fat, 22 mg Chol, 557 mg Sod, 70 g Carb, 10 g Fib, 21 g Prot, 207 mg Calc. **POINTS: 9.**

Caribbean Shrimp Salad

MAKES 4 SERVINGS

Jicama is so refreshing. Its sweet flavor and crunchy texture make it a natural addition to a salad. Choose a small jicama, since larger ones can be dry and fibrous.

2 cups mesclun
2 ruby-red grapefruits
1 pound medium shrimp, peeled, deveined, and cooked
2 kiwi fruits, peeled and sliced
1 small jicama, peeled and cut into strips
4 teaspoons extra-virgin olive oil
1 tablespoon chopped mint
1 tablespoon fresh lime juice
1 teaspoon honey
¼ teaspoon salt
Pinch cayenne

1. Line a platter with the mesclun. Peel and thinly slice the grapefruits over a bowl to catch the juice. Then arrange the grapefruit slices, shrimp, kiwi fruit slices, and jicama strips over the mesclun.
2. Whisk the oil, mint, lime juice, honey, salt, and cayenne into the grapefruit juice. Drizzle over the salad.

Per serving: 208 Cal, 6 g Fat, 1 g Sat Fat, 166 mg Chol, 337 mg Sod, 20 g Carb, 3 g Fib, 20 g Prot, 90 mg Calc. *POINTS: 4.*

shopping flash

Mesclun is a mixture of greens (including some that are very expensive or hard to find in most supermarkets, like red oak leaf lettuce or mâche). It's frequently sold already cleaned, but like all fresh vegetables, it should be rinsed well before serving.

California-Style Scallop Salad

MAKES 4 SERVINGS

This salad is so flavorful, it needs only a squeeze of fresh lemon and lime juice to dress it. It makes a lovely, light dinner on a balmy summer night.

¾ **pound scallops**

1½ **cups thawed frozen corn kernels**

1 **red bell pepper, seeded and diced**

1 **mango, peeled and diced**

½ **avocado, diced**

Juice of 1 lemon (2–3 tablespoons)

Juice of 1 lime (1–2 tablespoons)

4 **cups mesclun**

2 **tablespoons chopped cilantro (optional)**

1. Spray a medium nonstick skillet with nonstick cooking spray; heat. Sauté the scallops until just opaque, 3–4 minutes.

2. Meanwhile, in a medium bowl, mix the corn, bell pepper, mango, avocado, lemon juice, and lime juice. Add the scallops; toss to combine.

3. Divide the mesclun among 4 plates; top with the scallop salad, then sprinkle with the cilantro (if using).

Per serving: 204 Cal, 2 g Fat, 0 g Sat Fat, 28 mg Chol, 387 mg Sod, 33 g Carb, 4 g Fib, 18 g Prot, 65 mg Calc. **POINTS: 3.**

shopping flash

Purchase bay, calico, or sea scallops for this salad. It is also tasty with shrimp, crab, or surimi, or a combination of different types of seafood.

California-Style
Scallop Salad

Salmon Salad Niçoise

MAKES 4 SERVINGS

You can add almost anything to a niçoise salad, which gets its name from the French city of Nice. Other common additions include steamed green peas, tomato wedges, celery, artichoke hearts, radishes, or mushrooms. You can also garnish the salad with anchovy fillets and quartered hard-cooked eggs. We've used canned salmon instead of the traditional tuna for richer flavor and a calcium boost.

1¼ **pounds new potatoes, cut into bite-size chunks**
1 **teaspoon salt**
½ **pound green beans, trimmed**
1 **red bell pepper, seeded and thinly sliced**
½ **cucumber, peeled and thinly sliced**
½ **cup reduced-fat Italian salad dressing**
¼ **cup black olives, pitted and sliced**
4 **cups torn romaine lettuce leaves**
1 **(14½-ounce) can red or pink salmon, drained and flaked**
Freshly ground pepper

1. Place the potatoes in a large pot; add the salt and cold water to cover. Partially cover the pot and bring to a boil. Reduce the heat and cook until the potatoes are almost tender, about 8 minutes; add the green beans and cook until the potatoes are tender, about 4 minutes longer. Drain well.

2. In a large bowl, mix the bell pepper, cucumber, dressing, and olives. Add the potatoes and beans; toss to combine.

3. Arrange the lettuce on a platter or 4 plates. Top with the potato mixture, then chunks of the salmon; sprinkle with the pepper before serving.

Per serving: 301 Cal, 9 g Fat, 2 g Sat Fat, 57 mg Chol, 1,131 mg Sod, 29 g Carb, 6 g Fib, 26 g Prot, 292 mg Calc. *POINTS: 6*.

cooking flash

To make pitting the olives easier, gently smash them with the flat side of a chef's knife, or roll over them with a rolling pin. Prep the remaining vegetables while the potatoes cook.

Warm Mixed Seafood Salad

MAKES 4 SERVINGS

Although we like this combination of seafood, you could replace half of the shrimp with ¼ pound of cleaned calamari.

2 cups torn Boston or red-leaf lettuce
1 cup torn radicchio leaves
1 cup watercress leaves
2 tablespoons olive oil
½ pound medium shrimp, peeled and deveined
¼ pound sea scallops, halved, or bay scallops
¼ pound monkfish fillet, cut into 1-inch pieces
1 shallot, minced
2 tablespoons fresh lemon juice
Pinch salt
Freshly ground pepper, to taste
1 tablespoon water

1. Combine the lettuce, radicchio, and watercress in a bowl.
2. Heat 1½ teaspoons of the oil in a nonstick skillet, then add the shrimp, scallops, monkfish, and shallot. Sauté until the shrimp are pink. Remove from the heat and keep warm.
3. Combine the lemon juice, salt, pepper, and water with the remaining oil in a glass jar. Cover the jar and shake to blend. Pour half the dressing over the salad greens and toss to coat.
4. Divide the greens among 4 plates, then top with the seafood. Drizzle the salads with the remaining dressing.

Per serving: 190 Cal, 9 g Fat, 1 g Sat Fat, 107 mg Chol, 188 mg Sod, 4 g Carb, 0 g Fib, 23 g Prot, 81 mg Calc. *POINTS: 5.*

cooking flash

Watch the seafood closely as it cooks—scallops, especially, can go from tender to rubbery in seconds. Shrimp turn bright pinkish orange, so they're easiest to tell when done; scallops should be just opaque, with a bit of golden-brown crust at the edges.

Roast Pork, Orange, and Beet Salad

  MAKES 4 SERVINGS

The flavors in this salad hail from Mexico. The combination might sound unusual, but it is delectable. Although jarred beets work fine, roasted beets are superb. On a night when you have the time, wrap two or three trimmed small beets in foil and roast in a 400–425°F oven until tender (about an hour); cool slightly, then peel and slice.

2 **tablespoons red-wine vinegar**
2 **teaspoons vegetable oil**
½ **teaspoon salt**
4 **cups torn romaine lettuce**
2 **cups thinly sliced lean roasted pork loin**
2 **oranges, peeled and thinly sliced**
1 **red onion, thinly sliced**
2 **tablespoons minced cilantro**
½ **jalapeño pepper, seeded, deveined, and minced (wear gloves to prevent irritation)**
1 **cup sliced cooked beets**

1. Whisk the vinegar, oil, and salt in a small bowl.
2. Combine the lettuce, pork, oranges, onion, cilantro, and jalapeño in a bowl. Drizzle with the dressing and toss well to combine.
3. Divide the beets among 4 salad plates; top with the salad.

Per serving: 187 Cal, 6 g Fat, 2 g Sat Fat, 46 mg Chol, 338 mg Sod, 14 g Carb, 4 g Fib, 18 g Prot, 63 mg Calc. *POINTS: 3.*

shopping flash

For the most nutrition, opt for dark salad greens. Spinach, arugula, and green-leaf lettuce are higher in vital nutrients, like folate, than iceberg lettuce.

Roast Pork, Orange, and Beet Salad

Greek Salad

MAKES 2 SERVINGS

Feta cheese has a strong tangy flavor, but it's also high in fat and calories. Look for fat-free feta, which has the same flavor with a fraction of the calories. Feta coated with cracked black pepper or sun-dried tomatoes adds extra zip.

 2 **cups shredded romaine lettuce, plus**
   four leaves
½ **cucumber, peeled, seeded,**
   and chopped
 8 **cherry tomatoes, halved**
⅔ **cup crumbled fat-free feta cheese**
10 **kalamata olives, pitted and chopped**
 4 **teaspoons balsamic vinegar**
 2 **teaspoons extra-virgin olive oil**

Combine the shredded lettuce, cucumber, tomatoes, cheese, olives, vinegar, and oil in a bowl. Put the lettuce leaves on 2 plates; top with the salad.

Per serving: 197 Cal, 10 g Fat, 1 g Sat Fat, 7 mg Chol, 645 mg Sod, 12 g Carb, 3 g Fib, 15 g Prot, 646 mg Calc. *POINTS: 4.*

cooking flash

This salad makes a tasty sandwich, too. Simply heat a pocketless pita, top with the salad, and fold up; or heat a large pita, split in half, and fill.

Spinach Salad

MAKES 4 SERVINGS

This is the classic spinach salad, complete with bacon and hard-cooked egg. If you like, toss in some sliced white mushrooms or strips of roasted red pepper—or both.

2 tablespoons extra-virgin olive oil
2 tablespoons red-wine vinegar
1 teaspoon Dijon mustard
¼ teaspoon salt
Freshly ground pepper, to taste
1 (10-ounce) bag triple-washed
    spinach, rinsed and torn into
    bite-size pieces
2 slices bacon, crisp-cooked
    and crumbled
2 eggs, hard-cooked, peeled, and
    cut into wedges

In a large bowl, whisk the oil, vinegar, mustard, salt, and pepper. Add the spinach; toss to coat. Divide the salad among 4 plates, then sprinkle each serving with bacon and top with the eggs.

Per serving: 150 Cal, 12 g Fat, 2 g Sat Fat, 109 mg Chol, 365 mg Sod, 6 g Carb, 4 g Fib, 8 g Pro, 152 mg Calc. *POINTS: 3.*

Zippy Low-Fat Salad Add-Ins

1. Slices of Jerusalem artichokes or jicama add sweetness and crunch.
2. Sprouts will contribute texture and flavor: Try lentil, radish, and chickpea as well as the more common bean or alfalfa sprouts.
3. Fruit, like chopped Braeburn apple, sliced strawberries, or pineapple chunks, have sweet appeal.
4. A teaspoon of toasted chopped walnuts or sunflower seeds offers noticeable flavor and texture.
5. A tiny bit of full-flavored cheese, like feta, blue cheese, or chèvre (goat cheese), adds big taste.
6. Herb-y flavorful greens like arugula, watercress, and sorrel are elegant.
7. Chopped sun-dried tomatoes added to your vinaigrette—mmm!

savory soups & stews

Mussels in Tomato Broth

Mussels in Tomato Broth

MAKES 4 SERVINGS

Steaming mussels in a seasoned broth adds immeasurably to their flavor. This is a variation on the Italian classic Mussels in Acqua Pazza. To make the authentic version, add ¼ to ½ teaspoon crushed red pepper to the wine and omit the lemon zest.

4 teaspoons olive oil
1 small onion, chopped
4 garlic cloves, minced
3 plum tomatoes, coarsely chopped
1 cup dry white wine
2 teaspoons chopped flat-leaf parsley
1 teaspoon lemon zest strips
1 pound mussels, scrubbed
  and debearded

1. Heat a very large pot. Swirl in the oil, then add the onion and garlic. Sauté until golden, then add the tomatoes and cook until they start to break down. Add the wine, half of the parsley, and half of the lemon zest and bring to a boil. Add the mussels, reduce the heat, cover, and simmer until the mussels open, 6–8 minutes (discard any mussels that don't open).

2. Divide the mussels and broth among 4 soup bowls. Sprinkle with the remaining parsley and lemon zest and serve.

Per serving: 174 Cal, 7 g Fat, 1 g Sat Fat, 24 mg Chol, 252 mg Sod, 8 g Carb, 1 g Fib, 11 g Prot, 42 mg Calc. **POINTS: 4.**

shopping flash

Farm-raised mussels tend to be cleaner than their cousins from the wild, but you'll still have to pull off their beards. Plan to cook the mussels the day you buy them. For a little variety (and a colorful presentation) you might want to try green-tipped mussels, also called New Zealand mussels.

Hot "Gazpacho"

MAKES 4 SERVINGS

Although gazpacho means "uncooked" in the Andalusian dialect, this take on the Spanish classic is hot in both senses of the word: It's served warm, and the pepper sauce adds fire. Serve this zesty soup with crusty bread and alcohol-free sangría [see below].

1 **green bell pepper, seeded and chopped**
1 **small cucumber, peeled, seeded and sliced**
1 **onion, chopped**
3 **tomatoes, seeded and chopped**
¼ **cup packed cilantro leaves**
3 **cups spicy mixed vegetable juice**
2 **tablespoons red-wine vinegar**
1 **tablespoon olive oil**
1 **clove garlic, minced**
⅛ **teaspoon freshly ground pepper**
Hot red pepper sauce, to taste

In a food processor, finely chop the bell pepper, cucumber, and onion; transfer to a large nonreactive saucepan. In the food processor, finely chop the tomatoes and cilantro; add to the pepper mixture. Stir the vegetable juice, vinegar, oil, and garlic into the tomato mixture; add the ground pepper. Heat the soup to serving temperature, then add the pepper sauce.

Per serving: 129 Cal, 4 g Fat, 1 g Sat Fat, 0 mg Chol, 276 mg Sod, 21 g Carb, 4 g Fib, 4 g Prot, 74 mg Calc.
POINTS: 2.

cooking flash

To make an alcohol-free sangría: Combine a bottle of nonalcoholic red wine or grape juice with ¼ cup of orange juice, 1 tablespoon of sugar, orange and lemon slices, and apple wedges; chill overnight. Stir in 1 cup of club soda just before serving.

Chickpea and Swiss Chard Soup

MAKES 4 SERVINGS

Chickpeas have grown in Sicily since before recorded history. During the time of the Roman empire, they were imported throughout Italy. You'll find variations on this soup all over the Mediterranean.

4 teaspoons olive oil
1 onion, finely chopped
1 carrot, thinly sliced
1 celery stalk, thinly sliced
8 cups cleaned shredded Swiss chard leaves (about 1 bunch)
Pinch salt
¼ cup tomato puree
¾ cup canned chickpeas, rinsed and drained
2 cups low-sodium chicken broth
2 cups water
4 slices hearty peasant bread, toasted
1 teaspoon chopped fresh rosemary

1. Heat the oil in a nonstick saucepan, then add the onion, carrot, and celery. Sauté until the vegetables are softened. Add the chard and cook, stirring, until it wilts, then add the salt and tomato puree. Reduce the heat and simmer 10 minutes. Stir in the chickpeas, broth, and water and simmer 10 minutes longer.

2. Put 1 slice of toast in each of 4 bowls, then ladle in the soup; let stand a few minutes to soak the bread. Sprinkle with the rosemary and serve.

Per serving: 237 Cal, 9 g Fat, 1 g Sat Fat, 0 mg Chol, 571 mg Sod, 34 g Carb, 5 g Fib, 10 g Prot, 113 mg Calc. ***POINTS: 5.***

Tortellini in Garlic Broth with White Beans and Greens

MAKES 4 SERVINGS

We cook the tortellini separately and add it at the end to keep the broth from getting too starchy. Whether you use fresh or frozen tortellini, be sure to watch the time so it doesn't overcook.

3 cups fresh or frozen cheese tortellini

3½ cups vegetable or chicken broth

4 garlic cloves, minced

1 teaspoon dried sage or rosemary leaves, crumbled

2 cups coarsely chopped cleaned spinach or other greens

1 (16-ounce) can small white or navy beans, rinsed and drained

4 sun-dried tomatoes, minced

¼ cup grated Parmesan cheese

1. Cook the tortellini according to package directions, until just tender (do not overcook).

2. Meanwhile, in a large saucepan, bring the broth, garlic, sage, and 1 cup water to a boil. Stir in the spinach, beans, and tomatoes. Reduce the heat and simmer until the spinach and tomatoes are tender, about 5 minutes. Stir in the tortellini; simmer 1 minute longer. Sprinkle with the cheese and serve.

Per serving: 351 Cal, 4 g Fat, 2 g Sat Fat, 26 mg Chol, 967 mg Sod, 48 g Carb, 6 g Fib, 18 g Prot, 274 mg Calc. **POINTS: 6.**

shopping flash

It pays to invest in good Parmesan cheese, such as Parmigiano-Reggiano, because a little goes a long way in the flavor department. Buy a small wedge, cut it into smaller wedges, and keep them wrapped in plastic, then in foil, in the refrigerator or freezer. (It's a dry cheese, so it doesn't spoil as fast as other cheeses, and freezing won't compromise its texture.) Bring it to room temperature, then grate what you need by hand or in a food processor.

**Tortellini in Garlic Broth
with White Beans and Greens**

Escarole Soup

MAKES 4 SERVINGS

Chicken broth, escarole, and cheese combine to make a soup that's delicate yet rich in flavor. Even though it doesn't take much time to prepare, it tastes like it's been simmering all day. Serve this as a first course, as they would in Italy, or stir in some shredded chicken breast for a light meal.

1 head escarole, cleaned and chopped
¼ cup water
6 cups low-sodium chicken broth
4 teaspoons grated Parmesan cheese
Freshly ground pepper, to taste

1. Combine the escarole and water in a saucepan; cover and cook over low heat, checking frequently to be sure that some liquid remains and adding a little water if necessary, until the escarole is wilted and tender, about 5 minutes. Drain and squeeze out any excess liquid.
2. Bring the broth to a boil; add the escarole. Reduce the heat and simmer, stirring occasionally, until the escarole is very tender, 10 minutes. Sprinkle with the cheese and pepper and serve.

Per serving: 58 Cal, 4 g Fat, 2 g Sat Fat, 2 mg Chol, 226 mg Sod, 5 g Carb, 2 g Fib, 7 g Prot, 89 mg Calc. ***POINTS: 1.***

Give Canned Soups the Homemade Touch

- **Black bean soup:** Sprinkle on shredded reduced-fat cheddar cheese or chopped Canadian bacon.
- **Chicken noodle soup:** Toss in some fresh peas, as well as freshly chopped parsley or dill.
- **Reduced-fat or light cream of mushroom soup:** Add a touch of sherry.
- **Tomato soup:** Stir in cooked grains like barley or basmati rice.
- **Vegetable soup:** Add a cup of thawed frozen veggies.

Potato-Leek Soup

MAKES 4 CUPS

If you like, serve this soup cold—it's the classic way to serve vichyssoise (cold potato soup). Stir in a bit of broth if the soup has thickened too much.

1 tablespoon olive oil
3–4 leeks, cleaned and sliced
4 scallions, thinly sliced
4 cups vegetable broth
2 large all-purpose potatoes, peeled and chopped
⅓ cup fat-free sour cream
⅛ teaspoon ground white pepper
2 tablespoons snipped chives

1. Heat the oil in a nonstick saucepan, then add the leeks and scallions and sauté until barely softened, about 3 minutes. Add ⅓ cup of the broth, cover, and cook until the vegetables are tender, about 10 minutes.
2. Stir in the potatoes, then add another ⅔ cup of the broth and bring to a boil. Reduce the heat and simmer, partially covered, until the potatoes are softened, about 10 minutes.
3. Transfer the soup to a blender and puree. Remove the knob in the lid; with the machine running, gradually pour 2 more cups of broth through the hole. Return the puree to the saucepan and stir in the remaining cup of broth, the sour cream, and pepper. Heat to serving temperature. Sprinkle with the chives and serve.

Per serving: 213 Cal, 4 g Fat, 1 g Sat Fat, 0 mg Chol, 111 mg Sod, 41 g Carb, 6 g Fib, 6 g Prot, 66 mg Calc.
POINTS: 4.

Savory Sausage Stew

Savory Sausage Stew

MAKES 4 SERVINGS

This hearty stew is perfect on a chilly, rainy day. If you like, serve it steaming hot in big mugs with thick slices of multigrain bread for a casual, satisfying meal.

1 teaspoon vegetable oil
¾ pound Italian-style turkey sausage, casings removed
2 onions, chopped
1 turnip, peeled and chopped
½ carrot, sliced
1 celery stalk, sliced
4 new red potatoes, scrubbed and quartered
1 cup chicken broth
1 bay leaf
½ teaspoon dried thyme
¼ teaspoon dried sage
¼ teaspoon freshly ground pepper
½ small head green cabbage, cut into 4 wedges
1 teaspoon all-purpose flour, dissolved in 1 tablespoon cold water
¼ cup minced parsley
2 teaspoons cider vinegar

1. Heat the oil in a nonstick saucepan, then add the sausage, onions, turnip, carrot, and celery. Cook, breaking apart the sausage with a spoon, until the sausage is browned. Stir in the potatoes, broth, bay leaf, thyme, sage, and pepper; bring to a boil. Place the cabbage over the stew, then reduce the heat, cover, and simmer until the potatoes and cabbage are tender, about 15 minutes. With a slotted spoon, transfer the cabbage to a serving bowl.

2. Stir the dissolved flour into the stew; simmer, stirring frequently, until the liquid thickens slightly. With a slotted spoon, transfer the sausage and vegetables to the serving bowl; discard the bay leaf. Stir the parsley and vinegar into the liquid; pour over the sausage and vegetables.

Per serving: 260 Cal, 11 g Fat, 3 g Sat Fat, 50 mg Chol, 968 mg Sod, 25 g Carb, 4 g Fib, 19 g Prot, 87 mg Calc. *POINTS: 5.*

Stovetop Cassoulet

MAKES 4 SERVINGS

Cassoulet is a stew of meat and beans from the south of France that's traditionally baked for several hours at a low temperature. This quick version gets placed under the broiler for just a minute to finish it off. Cassoulet is one of those dishes that's even better made a day or two ahead and reheated.

¼ **pound hot Italian-style turkey sausage, cut into 1-inch slices**

¼ **pound skinless boneless chicken breast, cut into bite-size pieces**

¼ **pound precooked frozen sausage-and-rice links, thawed and cut into 1-inch slices**

1 **(15½-ounce) can small white beans, rinsed and drained**

1 **(14½-ounce) can diced tomatoes with garlic and onion**

¼ **cup tomato paste**

¼ **teaspoon dried thyme leaves, crumbled**

¼ **teaspoon dried rosemary leaves, crumbled**

¼ **teaspoon fennel seeds, crushed**

½ **cup fresh bread crumbs**

¼ **cup chopped parsley**

1. Preheat the broiler. In a large nonstick skillet, sauté the turkey sausage until browned, about 5 minutes. Add the chicken and sauté until browned, about 3 minutes longer. Stir in the sausage-and-rice links, beans, tomatoes, tomato paste, thyme, rosemary, fennel seeds, and ½ cup water. Simmer until most of the liquid evaporates, about 10 minutes.

2. Transfer to a 1-quart flameproof casserole. Mix the bread crumbs and parsley; sprinkle evenly over the casserole. Broil 4 inches from the heat until the crumbs are golden brown, 1–2 minutes.

Per serving: 364 Cal, 11 g Fat, 3 g Sat Fat, 62 mg Chol, 658 mg Sod, 41 g Carb, 9 g Fib, 28 g Prot, 158 mg Calc. *POINTS: 7.*

cooking flash

If you have a food processor, whirl the bread and parsley together to save a step. Crumbling dried herbs releases their flavor, and it makes the texture of spiny herbs like thyme and rosemary more palatable.

Tuscan Bean-and-Green Soup

MAKES 4 SERVINGS

Classic ingredients from Tuscany—white beans, rosemary, and spinach—are brought together in this quick and delicious soup. Serve it with Grilled Vegetable Sandwich wedges [page 49] for an easy supper.

1 **tablespoon olive oil**
3 **garlic cloves, minced**
1 **teaspoon rosemary leaves, crumbled**
¼ **teaspoon crushed red pepper**
1 **cup canned white beans, rinsed
  and drained**
½ **cup evaporated fat-free milk**
2 **tablespoons tomato paste**
½ **teaspoon salt**
¼ **teaspoon freshly ground pepper**
2 **cups water**
1 **carrot, thinly sliced**
2 **cups cleaned spinach leaves**
½ **cup roasted red peppers, drained
  and cut into strips**

1. Heat the oil in a saucepan, then add the garlic, rosemary, and crushed red pepper. Sauté until the garlic is fragrant, then stir in the beans, milk, tomato paste, salt, ground pepper, and water. Bring to a boil, then reduce the heat and simmer until the flavors are blended, about 10 minutes.

2. Transfer the soup to a blender or food processor and puree. Return to the saucepan and add the carrot; cook about 5 minutes, then add the spinach and roasted peppers. Cook, stirring, until the spinach is wilted.

Per serving: 173 Cal, 5 g Fat, 1 g Sat Fat, 1 mg Chol, 382 mg Sod, 24 g Carb, 4 g Fib, 9 g Prot, 186 mg Cal. *POINTS: 3.*

cooking flash

If you don't have a blender or food processor, or if you simply prefer a chunkier texture, mash some of the beans with a potato masher or the back of a large spoon instead of pureeing the soup.

Chicken Soup with Rice

MAKES 6 SERVINGS

Arborio rice has a high starch content that thickens the soup as it cooks. Any short-grain Italian, Spanish, or Japanese rice can be substituted for Arborio.

2 **teaspoons olive oil**
2 **carrots, diced**
2 **celery stalks, diced**
1 **onion, chopped**
5 **cups low-sodium chicken broth**
⅔ **cup Arborio rice**
1½ **cups diced cooked chicken breast**
1 **head escarole, cleaned and shredded**
Salt, to taste
Freshly ground pepper, to taste

1. Heat the oil in a nonstick saucepan, then add the carrots, celery, and onion. Sauté until the onion is translucent. Stir in the broth and bring to a boil. Reduce the heat, stir in the rice, and simmer, covered, 15 minutes. Stir in the chicken, cover, and cook until the rice is tender and the chicken is heated through, about 3 minutes. **2.** Remove the pot from the heat and stir in the escarole; cover and set aside until the escarole wilts, about 2 minutes. Stir in the salt and pepper.

Per serving: 213 Cal, 4 g Fat, 1 g Sat Fat, 27 mg Chol, 150 mg Sod, 29 g Carb, 4 g Fib, 15 g Prot, 86 mg Calc. *POINTS: 4.*

Velvety Chicken, Corn, and Coconut Soup

 MAKES 4 SERVINGS

This hearty soup is Chinese in inspiration. The cream-style corn provides an ultrarich silky-smooth texture and subtly sweet flavor. Serve it with steamed vegetable dumplings from your favorite Chinese restaurant.

3 tablespoons rice wine or dry sherry
1 tablespoon grated peeled fresh ginger
1 teaspoon salt
10 ounces skinless boneless chicken breast, cubed
6 cups low-sodium chicken broth
3 cups cream-style corn
¼ cup shredded coconut
2 tablespoons cornstarch, dissolved in ¼ cup water
3 scallions, minced
2 teaspoons Asian (dark) sesame oil

1. Combine the wine, ginger, and ¼ teaspoon of the salt in a large bowl. Add the chicken and toss to coat.
2. Bring the broth to a boil in a saucepan. Stir in the corn, coconut, and the remaining ¾ teaspoon salt. Return to a boil, then add the chicken with its marinade. Reduce the heat, cover, and simmer until the chicken is cooked through. Bring the soup back to a boil, then add the dissolved cornstarch and cook, stirring constantly, until the soup thickens slightly. Stir in the scallions and sesame oil.

Per serving: 331 Cal, 9 g Fat, 3 g Sat Fat, 41 mg Chol, 1,331 mg Sod, 45 g Carb, 3 g Fib, 25 g Prot, 54 mg Calc. *POINTS: 7.*

cooking flash

Asian sesame oil is made from toasted sesame seeds. It is quite dark and has a distinctive flavor. Some cooks believe it develops an unpleasant taste at high heat, so it's best to stir it in at the end of cooking or cook it over a low flame.

Pork and Noodle Soup

MAKES 4 SERVINGS

Here's the grown-up version of the chicken noodle soup you loved as a kid. Our superfast version can be ready in about the time it takes to boil water, and it's not much more difficult. For a vegetarian version, use all vegetable broth and substitute cubes of firm tofu for the pork.

2 **cups low-sodium vegetable broth**
2 **cups low-sodium chicken broth**
2 **cups low-sodium beef broth**
¼ **pound cooked lean pork, cubed**
¼ **pound capellini**
2 **teaspoons Asian (dark) sesame oil**
6 **scallions, thinly sliced on the diagonal**

1. Bring the broths to a boil in a saucepan. Reduce the heat and add the pork; simmer until heated through.

2. Meanwhile, cook the capellini according to package directions. Drain and toss with the oil, then divide among 4 bowls. Ladle in the broth, then sprinkle with the scallions and serve.

Per serving: 199 Cal, 7 g Fat, 2 g Sat Fat, 22 mg Chol, 241 mg Sod, 20 g Carb, 1 g Fib, 16 g Prot, 35 mg Calc. *POINTS: 4.*

Reheating Tips

• Don't recook soup when reheating; bring it to a slow simmer and serve immediately.

• Refresh soups by thinning with broth or water when reheating. (This is especially important for bean and grain soups.)

• Add a little salt and extra seasonings when reheating, since soups may lose some of their flavor when refrigerated.

• Skim the fat (which will solidify during refrigeration) from the surface of soups with a slotted spoon before reheating.

• Volatile flavors can change in the freezer. If you plan to freeze part of a big batch of soup, remove the amount you plan to freeze before you add seasonings like liquor or vinegars, lemon, chiles, or garlic. Add these ingredients after the frozen soup is thawed.

Thai Hot and Sour Fish Soup

MAKES 4 SERVINGS

Thai chiles are sometimes called bird chiles—a reference to their shape, which is similar to a bird's beak. No Thai chiles at your market? Use jalapeño peppers instead.

½ **cup rice**
5 **cups low-sodium chicken broth**
2 **(1½-inch) Thai red or green chiles,**
    seeded, deveined, and minced (wear
    gloves to prevent irritation)
3 **tablespoons rice vinegar**
1 **tablespoon fresh lime juice**
Pinch sugar
2 **cups julienned peeled daikon**
1¼ **pounds sea bass fillets, cut**
    into ¾-inch strips
3 **tablespoons minced cilantro**

1. Cook the rice according to package directions. When it is done, form it into 4 balls and set each in a soup bowl.
2. Meanwhile, combine 2 tablespoons of the broth, the chiles, vinegar, lime juice, and sugar in a bowl.
3. Bring the remaining broth to a boil in a saucepan. Reduce the heat, add the daikon, and simmer until tender, about 5 minutes. Stir in the chile mixture and fish; simmer until the fish is cooked through, about 5 minutes longer. Ladle over the rice, sprinkle with the cilantro, and serve.

Per serving: 285 Cal, 6 g Fat, 2 g Sat Fat, 58 mg Chol, 251 mg Sod, 28 g Carb, 0 g Fib, 33 g Prot, 57 mg Calc. *POINTS : 6.*

Chinese Seafood Soup

MAKES 4 SERVINGS

Chinese cooks use many different types of cabbages. Bok choy, a staple, is sometimes sold under the name Chinese cabbage. To make things even more confusing, Napa cabbage occasionally goes by the same name. Bok choy has bright green leaves and white stalks. Napa has paler green leaves.

6 **ounces spaghetti**
4 **cups low-sodium chicken broth**
3 **cups thinly sliced bok choy**
2 **tablespoons reduced-sodium**
  soy sauce
2 **tablespoons rice vinegar**
3 **garlic cloves, minced**
½ **pound clams, scrubbed and soaked**
¼ **pound cockles, soaked**
½ **pound medium shrimp, peeled**
  and deveined
4 **scallions, thinly sliced**
1 **teaspoon Asian (dark) sesame oil**

1. Cook the spaghetti according to package directions. Drain and keep warm.
2. Bring the broth, bok choy, soy sauce, vinegar, and garlic to a boil in a saucepan. Add the clams and cockles. Reduce the heat, cover, and simmer about 3 minutes; then add the shrimp, cover again, and simmer until the clams and cockles open and the shrimp turn pink, about 2 minutes longer (discard any clams or cockles that don't open). Stir in the scallions, sesame oil, and the spaghetti before serving.

Per serving: 321 Cal, 7 g Fat, 2 g Sat Fat, 136 mg Chol, 547 mg Sod, 39 g Carb, 2 g Fib, 144 mg Calc. *POINTS: 7.*

shopping flash

Use any variety of hard-shelled clams you prefer: Littlenecks, cherrystones, or chowder clams would all work fine in this recipe. Cockles are small bivalves with ribbed shells. If you can't find them, simply omit them from the recipe and use a bit more clams.

Chinese Seafood Soup

Zesty Red Clam Chowder

MAKES 4 SERVINGS

At the famed Oyster Bar in New York City's Grand Central Station, the cognoscenti order "red" or "white" clam chowder instead of Manhattan or New England. Use less cayenne pepper, if you prefer.

1 onion, diced

3 slices bacon, diced

2 (6½-ounce) cans minced clams
   (do not drain)

1 large all-purpose potato, peeled
   and chopped

1 celery stalk, chopped

1 (14½-ounce) can whole tomatoes

1 cup canned crushed tomatoes

2 tablespoons chopped parsley

1 teaspoon dried oregano, crumbled

½ teaspoon salt

½ teaspoon cayenne pepper, or to taste

¼ teaspoon freshly ground pepper

1. In a large nonstick saucepan or Dutch oven, sauté the onion and bacon until the onion is tender and the bacon is browned, about 10 minutes.

2. Stir in the clams, potato, celery, and 1 cup water; bring to a boil. Reduce the heat and simmer until the potato is tender, about 10 minutes. Stir in the whole tomatoes, crushed tomatoes, parsley, oregano, salt, cayenne, and pepper; cook, breaking apart the whole tomatoes with a wooden spoon, until heated through, about 5 minutes.

Per serving: 176 Cal, 10 g Fat, 4 g Sat Fat, 14 mg Chol, 816 mg Sod, 18 g Carb, 3 g Fib, 5 g Prot, 76 mg Calc. **POINTS: 4.**

cooking flash

If you have time, use two dozen fresh little-neck clams, shucked, instead of the canned clams.

If you prefer New England clam chowder, use 2 to 3 cups of milk instead of the whole and crushed tomatoes; omit the oregano and cayenne.

Beef and Vegetable Soup

MAKES 4 SERVINGS

This soup is both light and flavorful, and it adapts well to any combination of vegetables. Feel free to substitute your favorites or whatever's most abundant in the garden.

1 teaspoon olive oil
1 onion, chopped
2 celery stalks, chopped
2 carrots, peeled and chopped
10 ounces lean boneless beef loin, cut into ½-inch cubes
1 cup low-sodium beef broth
1 cup chopped green beans
1 cup thawed frozen corn kernels
3 scallions, sliced
¼ cup chopped flat-leaf parsley
¼ teaspoon freshly ground pepper
2 cups water

Heat the oil in a nonstick saucepan, then add the onion, celery, carrots, and beef. Sauté until the beef is browned. Add the broth, beans, corn, scallions, parsley, pepper, and water and bring to a boil. Reduce the heat and simmer, stirring occasionally, until the vegetables are tender.

Per serving: 194 Cal, 5 g Fat, 2 g Sat Fat, 42 mg Chol, 120 mg Sod, 19 g Carb, 4 g Fib, 19 g Prot, 53 mg Calc. *POINTS: 3.*

Vegetable Paprikash

MAKES 4 SERVINGS

If your jar of paprika doesn't specify "hot" or "sweet," it's probably the latter. For the best flavor, use authentic Hungarian paprika, which comes in a rectangular tin. Be warned: Hot paprika is very hot! If that's all you have, start with ½ teaspoon and add more to taste.

2 teaspoons olive oil
1 onion, chopped
2 garlic cloves, chopped
2 turnips, peeled and chopped
1 (16-ounce) bag baby carrots
½ cup water
1 (8-ounce) package sliced mushrooms
1 tablespoon sweet paprika
½ teaspoon salt
½ teaspoon caraway seeds
1 (15-ounce) can white beans,
  rinsed and drained
1 (14½-ounce) can diced
  tomatoes, drained
2 tablespoons tomato paste
¼ cup light sour cream
2 teaspoons minced dill
6 ounces wide egg noodles

1. Heat a nonstick skillet. Swirl in the oil, then add the onion and garlic. Sauté until golden, then add the turnips, carrots, and water. Bring to a boil. Reduce the heat slightly, cover, and cook until the turnips are fork-tender, about 10 minutes. Stir in the mushrooms and simmer, covered, until they are tender, about 5 minutes longer. Stir in the paprika, salt, and caraway seeds, then add the beans, tomatoes, and tomato paste. Bring back to a boil, then reduce the heat, cover, and simmer until slightly thickened. Remove from the heat and stir in the sour cream and dill.

2. Meanwhile, cook the noodles according to package directions. Drain and divide the noodles among 4 plates, then top with the vegetable mixture.

Per serving: 469 Cal, 7 g Fat, 2 g Sat Fat, 45 mg Chol, 367 mg Sod, 83 g Carb, 11 g Fib, 22 g Pro, 189 mg Calc.
POINTS: 9.

Vegetable Tagine

MAKES 4 SERVINGS

A tagine is a Moroccan stew. It gets its name from the vessel it's cooked in, a shallow pot with a high cone-shaped lid. Tagines are commonly served with couscous. Minted peas would be a lovely side dish.

2 **teaspoons olive oil**
1 **pound new potatoes, scrubbed**
 and halved
2 **cups cauliflower florets**
1 **(16-ounce) can chickpeas, rinsed**
 and drained
1 **cup water**
1 **carrot, cut into chunks**
8 **dried apricot halves, chopped**
1 **tablespoon fresh lemon juice**
1 **teaspoon ground coriander**
1 **teaspoon sweet paprika**
½ **teaspoon ground cumin**
½ **teaspoon ground ginger**
½ **teaspoon salt**
½ **teaspoon freshly ground pepper**

In a large pot, swirl in the oil and heat. Sauté the potatoes until golden brown, then stir in the remaining ingredients and bring to a boil. Reduce the heat, cover, and simmer until the vegetables are tender, 15–20 minutes.

Per serving: 257 Cal, 5 g Fat, 0 g Sat Fat, 0 mg Chol, 565 mg Sod, 48 g Carb, 11 g Fib, 8 g Pro, 69 mg Calc. *POINTS: 5.*

Grilled Vegetable Sandwich

pizza, sandwiches, & wraps

Grilled Vegetable Sandwich

MAKES 6 SERVINGS

Use a prebaked pizza crust shell or a prepared focaccia shell for this easy sandwich; look for them in your supermarket's bread section.

1 small zucchini, quartered lengthwise

1 small crookneck squash, quartered lengthwise

1 portobello mushroom, cut into 6 pieces

1 (7-ounce) jar roasted red peppers, rinsed and drained

1 tablespoon reduced-fat mayonnaise

½ tablespoon oregano leaves

½ tablespoon thyme leaves

1 garlic clove, peeled

1 (8-inch) prebaked pizza crust or focaccia shell, halved horizontally

4 slices provolone cheese

1. Preheat the broiler. Arrange the zucchini, squash, and mushroom in a single layer on a baking sheet and spray with nonstick spray. Broil until well browned, about 9 minutes. Remove and set the vegetables aside. Reduce the oven temperature to 450°F.

2. Puree the roasted peppers, mayonnaise, oregano, thyme, and garlic in a food processor. Place one half of the crust on the baking sheet. Spread the roasted pepper puree over it and layer with the vegetables, then the cheese. Top with the other half. Bake until the cheese melts and the sandwich is heated through, about 5 minutes. Cut into 6 wedges and serve.

Per serving: 183 Cal, 5 g Fat, 2 g Sat Fat, 10 mg Chol, 466 mg Sod, 27 g Carb, 2 g Fib, 8 g Prot, 100 mg Calc. *POINTS: 4.*

cooking flash

If you'd rather not turn on the broiler, you could grill the vegetables for 9 minutes in a ridged grill pan over high heat.

Lamb Burgers with Feta

MAKES 4 SERVINGS

Lamb burgers are a flavorful change from beef burgers. If you don't see ground lamb at your supermarket, ask the butcher to grind some for you. A salad of sliced cucumbers in a yogurt–dill dressing and warmed pitas complete the meal.

1 pound lean ground lamb
1 teaspoon salt
½ teaspoon garlic powder
2 teaspoons rosemary leaves, minced
Pinch freshly ground pepper
6 tablespoons crumbled feta cheese

1. Combine the lamb, salt, garlic powder, rosemary, and pepper. Form into 4 burgers.
2. Cook the burgers in a nonstick skillet until browned, about 5 minutes, then turn over and sprinkle with the cheese. Cover and cook until the cheese melts and the burgers are cooked through, about 3 minutes longer.

Per serving: 238 Cal, 11 g Fat, 6 g Sat Fat, 102 mg Chol, 748 mg Sod, 0 g Carb, 0 g Fib, 14 g Prot, 39 mg Calc. ***POINTS: 6.***

5 in a Flash!

In the what's-for-dinner doldrums and stumped for new ideas? Try these easy meals-in-minutes.

1. **Burger Party** Let the family make their own, by setting out cooked soy burgers, sourdough rolls, sliced plum tomatoes, pickles, low-fat cheese slices, and freshly washed arugula. Round out the meal with a big bowl of cole slaw blend tossed with your favorite fat-free dressing.

2. **Super-Dog Dinner** Top soy or turkey hot dogs with sautéed onions, sauerkraut, and some grainy mustard. Serve with a side of vegetarian baked beans.

3. **Asian Chicken Supreme** On individual sheets of aluminum foil, place a chicken breast with frozen Japanese-style vegetables, then splash with a dash of orange juice, teriyaki sauce, and grated ginger; fold the foil into a loose packet. Bake at 425°F until cooked through, about 20 minutes. Serve with rice.

4. **Goin' Fishin'** Make a light seafood salad by mixing surimi with fat-free mayonnaise, celery, and onion. Serve with a mesclun salad and whole-grain bread.

5. **"Where's the Meat?" Dinner** Instead of ground beef, heat frozen prebrowned vegetable protein crumbles and season with taco spice mix. Serve in taco shells with shredded lettuce, chopped tomato, and onion for a quick, spicy supper.

Antipasto Pizza

MAKES 6 SERVINGS

We've taken the typical components of an antipasto platter and used them to top a pizza. To crumble Parmesan, buy a block of cheese and chisel it into small chunks with a cheese knife or a fork.

1 (10-ounce) thin-crust pizza shell

1 cup spinach leaves, cleaned and chopped

1 (7-ounce) jar roasted red peppers, drained and sliced

6 canned artichoke hearts, drained and quartered

¼ cup crumbled Parmesan cheese

Preheat the oven to 450°F. Spray a baking sheet with nonstick cooking spray. Set the pizza shell on the baking sheet. Arrange the spinach evenly on the shell, then top with the red peppers and artichokes and sprinkle with the cheese. Bake until lightly browned, 10–12 minutes.

Per serving: 151 Cal, 3 g Fat, 1 g Sat Fat, 3 mg Chol, 474 mg Sod, 24 g Carb, 1 g Fib, 6 g Prot, 72 mg Calc. *POINTS: 3.*

California Pizza for One

MAKES 1 SERVING

You know those nights: You get home so late that everyone else has eaten and you're famished. But don't fall into the trap of eating whatever's around. A tasty dinner is just moments away—really!—with this speedy pizza.

1 (6-inch) pocketless pita
1 plum tomato, chopped
⅓ cup chopped cooked skinless chicken breast
3 tablespoons shredded Monterey jack cheese
⅛ avocado, diced
¼ cup alfalfa sprouts
2 tablespoons fat-free sour cream

Preheat the oven to 425°F. Set the pita on a baking sheet. Sprinkle with the tomato, chicken, and cheese, then bake until the cheese melts and the pita begins to get crisp, about 10 minutes. Sprinkle with the avocado and sprouts and dollop with the sour cream.

Per serving: 393 Cal, 3 g Fat, 5 g Sat Fat, 58 mg Chol, 495 mg Sod, 39 g Carb, 2 g Fib, 29 g Prot, 246 mg Calc. *POINTS: 8.*

cooking flash

If you have a toaster oven, use it to make this recipe even speedier. Because toaster ovens are small, you don't have to wait very long for them to preheat.

Cajun Shrimp Pizza

MAKES 8 SERVINGS

Some fish markets will peel and devein shrimp for you, either while you wait or if you call ahead. Be careful when you buy precleaned shrimp, though; if they were peeled soon after they were caught and then frozen, they may be very watery.

2 **teaspoons olive oil**
1 **onion, diced**
½ **cup seeded diced green bell pepper**
1 **celery stalk, coarsely chopped**
2 **garlic cloves, minced**
1 **(8-ounce) jar Spanish-style tomato sauce**
1 **bay leaf**
½ **teaspoon dried oregano**
½ **teaspoon dried thyme**
   Pinch cayenne
¼ **cup water**
1 **(10-ounce) thin-crust pizza shell**
1 **pound small shrimp, peeled and deveined**
¾ **cup shredded part-skim mozzarella cheese**

1. Preheat the oven to 450°F.
2. Heat the oil in a nonstick skillet. Sauté the onion, bell pepper, celery, and garlic until softened, then stir in the tomato sauce, bay leaf, oregano, thyme, cayenne, and water. Bring to a boil, then reduce the heat and simmer, stirring occasionally, until thickened. Discard the bay leaf.
3. Put the pizza shell on a baking sheet or pizza pan. Spoon the tomato sauce over the crust to within ½ inch of the edge, then top with the shrimp and cheese. Bake 5 minutes, until the shrimp are pink and the cheese melts.

Per serving: 204 Cal, 5 g Fat, 2 g Sat Fat, 92 mg Chol, 469 mg Sod, 22 g Carb, 1 g Fib, 18 g Prot, 116 mg Calc. *POINTS: 4.*

Greek Pizza

MAKES 4 SERVINGS

You can find prepared pizza dough at the supermarket (in cardboard tubes in the refrigerator case or with the frozen foods), but you might want to ask your favorite pizzeria whether they sell dough.

½ **pound pizza dough**
1 **tomato, sliced**
½ **green bell pepper, seeded and sliced**
½ **red onion, thinly sliced**
¾ **cup crumbled feta cheese (about 3 ounces)**
6 **large kalamata olives, pitted and quartered**
1 **teaspoon dried oregano**
¼ **teaspoon freshly ground pepper**

1. Preheat the oven to 450°F.
2. Sprinkle a counter lightly with flour, then turn the dough in the flour to coat. Stretch or roll the dough to a 10- to 12-inch circle, then transfer to a nonstick pizza pan or baking sheet. Top the dough with the tomato, bell pepper, onion, feta, olives, oregano, and ground pepper. Bake until the crust is browned and crisp, 15–20 minutes.

Per serving: 253 Cal, 9 g Fat, 4 g Sat Fat, 19 mg Chol, 788 mg Sod, 32 g Carb, 2 g Fib, 8 g Prot, 123 mg Calc.
POINTS: 5.

Barbecued Chicken Sandwiches

MAKES 4 SERVINGS

To shred chicken, put a cooked breast on a cutting board and use two forks to pull it into pieces.

2 cups shredded cooked chicken breasts
¼ cup barbecue sauce
¼ teaspoon chili powder
4 hamburger buns, split

Combine the chicken, barbecue sauce, and chili powder in a saucepan and heat to serving temperature. Spoon into the hamburger buns.

Per serving: 273 Cal, 8 g Fat, 2 g Sat Fat, 59 mg Chol, 419 mg Sod, 24 g Carb, 1 g Fib, 25 g Prot, 73 mg Calc. *POINTS: 6*

shopping flash

If you don't have leftover chicken, buy a package of chopped cooked chicken; they come in an array of flavors. An 8-ounce package will yield about 2 cups of chicken meat.

Sausage-and-Pepper Heroes

MAKES 4 SERVINGS

Sweet onions are usually bigger than common yellow onions; cutting the onion in half before slicing it lessens the unwieldiness of eating the larger slices. If you find small sweet onions, use two and just slice them into thin rings.

½ **pound Italian-style turkey sausage, cut into ½-inch slices**
1 **sweet onion, halved lengthwise and thinly sliced**
1 **teaspoon olive oil**
1 **red bell pepper, seeded and thinly sliced**
1 **green bell pepper, seeded and thinly sliced**
1 **tablespoon balsamic vinegar**
1 **(8-ounce) loaf Italian bread**

1. In a large nonstick skillet, sauté the sausage until browned, about 5 minutes. Add the onion and oil; sauté until softened, about 5 minutes longer. Transfer to a plate.
2. In the skillet, sauté the bell peppers until softened, about 5 minutes; if necessary, add up to 4 tablespoons water to prevent peppers from sticking. Stir in the vinegar, then return the sausage mixture to the skillet; toss to combine.
3. Split the bread lengthwise almost all the way through; spread open. Top with the sausage mixture. Close the bread, then cut crosswise into 4 sandwiches.

Per serving: 303 Cal, 8 g Fat, 2 g Sat Fat, 30 mg Chol, 780 mg Sod, 42 g Carb, 3 g Fib, 17 g Prot, 79 mg Calc.
POINTS: 6.

Sausage-and-
Pepper Heroes

Cobb Salad Sandwiches

MAKES 2 SERVINGS

To get the classic cobb salad flavor without the fuss of fresh blue cheese, we used blue cheese dressing. If you happen to have some blue cheese on hand, feel free to crumble some in; let it come to room temperature to make crumbling easier.

2 large sourdough pitas, halved

2 tablespoons reduced-calorie blue cheese dressing

4 thin slices lean deli turkey breast

2 slices bacon, crisp-cooked, drained, and broken into pieces

4 romaine lettuce leaves

1 tomato, thinly sliced

Spread the inside of each pita with ½ tablespoon of dressing; layer with the turkey, bacon, lettuce, and tomato. Drizzle with the remaining dressing.

Per serving: 326 Cal, 6 g Fat, 1 g Sat Fat, 16 mg Chol, 990 mg Sod, 57 g Carb, 5 g Fib, 15 g Prot, 122 mg Calc. *POINTS: 6.*

shopping flash

If you're looking to buy blue cheese, Roquefort—the Rolls Royce of blue cheese—is a bit pricey but worth every penny. It's strongly flavored, so a little goes a long, flavorful way.

Mozzarella in Carrozza

MAKES 4 SERVINGS

The name of this dish means "mozzarella in a carriage." In Italy, this is often served in a marinara or anchovy sauce. Our simpler rendition mixes anchovy into the sandwich filling.

¾ **cup grated skim-milk mozzarella**
6 **anchovy fillets, rinsed, patted dry,**
   and coarsely chopped
2 **tablespoons minced flat-leaf parsley**
2 **teaspoons olive oil**
2 **teaspoons fresh lemon juice**
1 **garlic clove, minced**
1 **(8-ounce) loaf Italian bread, cut**
   on the diagonal into 8 slices
1 **egg**
¼ **cup fat-free milk**

1. Combine the mozzarella, anchovies, parsley, oil, lemon juice, and garlic. Divide the mixture among 4 slices of bread, then top with the remaining 4 slices.

2. Spray a nonstick skillet with nonstick spray and set over medium-low heat.

3. Whisk the egg and milk in a shallow bowl until blended. Dip the sandwiches into the egg mixture, then transfer them to the skillet. Cook until the cheese melts and the egg is browned, about 3 minutes on each side, and serve.

Per serving: 268 Cal, 10 g Fat, 3 g Sat Fat, 69 mg Chol, 675 mg Sod, 30 g Carb, 2 g Fib, 14 g Prot, 224 mg Calc. **POINTS: 6.**

Chicken and Black Bean Tacos

MAKES 4 SERVINGS

Since taco shells typically pack three grams of fat per serving, we make fat-free taco shells for this dish.

4 **(6-inch) fat-free flour tortillas**

½ **pound skinless boneless chicken breast, cut into strips**

1 **cup canned black beans, rinsed and drained**

¼ **cup salsa**

2 **plum tomatoes, chopped**

1 **cup shredded lettuce**

2 **scallions, thinly sliced**

½ **cup shredded sharp cheddar cheese**

2 **tablespoons fat-free sour cream**

1. Preheat the oven to 450°F. Spray a nonstick baking sheet with nonstick cooking spray. Crumple 2 large sheets of aluminum foil into two 4-inch-high, 12-inch-long rectangles and place on the baking sheet. Drape the tortillas over the foil to form taco shells. Bake until golden, about 8 minutes. Let cool over the foil about 5 minutes.

2. Meanwhile, brown the chicken in a nonstick skillet. Stir in the black beans and salsa and heat to serving temperature. Fill the taco shells with the chicken mixture, then top the tacos with the tomatoes, lettuce, scallions, cheese, and sour cream. Serve immediately.

Per serving: 341 Cal, 8 g Fat, 3 g Sat Fat, 40 mg Chol, 751 mg Sod, 44 g Carb, 5 g Fib, 25 g Prot, 172 mg Calc. *POINTS: 7.*

Chicken Enchiladas

MAKES 4 SERVINGS

To make vegetarian enchiladas, simply replace the chicken with diced firm tofu.

1 (11-ounce) jar salsa
1 cup shredded cooked chicken breast
1 cup reduced-fat shredded
   Mexican cheese blend
¾ cup plain fat-free yogurt
1 small yellow squash, diced
3 tablespoons canned diced
   jalapeño peppers
8 (6-inch) corn tortillas
2 tablespoons minced parsley

1. Preheat the oven to 400°F. Spread ⅓ cup of the salsa in the bottom of a 10 x 6-inch baking dish. Mix the chicken, ½ cup of the cheese, ½ cup of the yogurt, the squash, and jalapeños in a bowl.

2. Heat the tortillas according to package directions. Spread about ¼ cup of the chicken mixture down the center of each tortilla. Roll up and place seam-side down in the baking dish. Pour the remaining salsa over the tortillas, then sprinkle with the remaining ½ cup of cheese. Cover with foil and bake until the cheese melts, about 20 minutes. Top with the remaining ¼ cup of yogurt, sprinkle with the parsley, and serve.

Per serving: 215 Cal, 3 g Fat, 1 g Sat Fat, 10 mg Chol, 588 mg Sod, 39 g Carb, 5 g Fib, 10 g Prot, 235 mg Calc. *POINTS: 4.*

cooking flash

If you have a microwave, it can make short work of heating a stack of tortillas. Just follow the directions on the package label.

Chicken Chilaquiles

MAKES 4 SERVINGS

Chilaquiles, tortilla strips layered with cheese, salsa, and meat, is a favorite dish in Mexico—and a popular way to use leftovers.

1 **large onion, thinly sliced and separated into rings**

6 **(6-inch) corn tortillas, cut into ½-inch strips**

½ **pound cooked skinless boneless chicken breast, cut into strips**

2 **tomatoes, chopped**

1 **(11-ounce) jar salsa**

¾ **cup low-sodium chicken broth**

¾ **cup grated reduced-fat cheddar cheese**

1. Preheat the oven to 400°F. Spray a 9 x 13-inch baking dish with nonstick spray.

2. Spray a nonstick skillet with nonstick spray and set over medium–high heat. Sauté the onion until softened.

3. Put half of the tortillas in the baking dish, covering the bottom (overlap the strips if necessary). Top with half of the chicken, half of the tomatoes, half of the onion, and half of the salsa, then repeat the layers. Pour in the broth. Cover with foil and bake 15 minutes. Sprinkle with the cheese and bake, uncovered, until the cheese melts, about 5 minutes longer.

Per serving: 296 Cal, 8 g Fat, 4 g Sat Fat, 6 mg Chol, 937 mg Sod, 31 g Carb, 4 g Fib, 28 g Prot, 276 mg Calc. **POINTS: 6.**

cooking flash

Serve this with a salad of black beans, corn, and chopped red onion. Dress the salad with a simple Mexican vinaigrette made of olive oil, red-wine vinegar, chili powder, and cilantro.

Sausage Rolls

MAKES 4 SERVINGS

Sausage rolls are a perfect on-the-run bite. If you're serving a sit-down meal, remove the sausage casings and break up the meat when you sauté it. If you like, add a sliced red or green bell pepper with the onion.

1 teaspoon extra-virgin olive oil
1 onion, sliced
4 low-fat Italian-style turkey sausages
8 (12 x 17-inch) sheets phyllo dough, at room temperature
½ teaspoon butter, melted

1. Preheat the oven to 375°F. Spray a baking sheet with nonstick spray. Heat the oil in a nonstick skillet. Sauté the onion until it just begins to brown, then add the sausages and cook, turning as needed, until the sausages are browned and the onion softened, 10–15 minutes longer.

2. Place the sheets of phyllo on a work surface and cover them with a damp paper towel. Remove 2 sheets and spray with butter-flavored nonstick spray. Remove 2 more sheets, lay them directly on top, and spray them. Cut the rectangle into two 12 x 8½-inch rectangles. Put 1 sausage and one-fourth of the onion in the center of each and roll the phyllo to cover the sausage. Repeat with the remaining phyllo, sausage, and onion. Transfer the sausage rolls to the baking sheet and brush with the butter. Bake until golden brown, 15–20 minutes.

Per serving: 221 Cal, 8 g Fat, 2 g Sat Fat, 37 mg Chol, 696 mg Sod, 24 g Carb, 1 g Fib, 12 g Prot, 11 mg Calc. *POINTS: 5.*

Asian Beef in Lettuce Wrappers

Asian Beef in Lettuce Wrappers

MAKES 4 SERVINGS

The dipping sauce in this recipe may be made up to three days ahead and refrigerated; prepare extra to use as a dipping sauce for crudités.

¼ **cup rice vinegar**
1 **tablespoon reduced-sodium soy sauce**
2 **teaspoons chopped mint leaves**
1 **teaspoon grated peeled fresh ginger**
1 **teaspoon grated orange zest**
1 **teaspoon Asian (dark) sesame oil**
8 **large red leaf lettuce leaves**
½ **pound lean roast beef, cut into thin strips**
1 **cup bean sprouts**
1 **kirby cucumber, grated**
Mint leaves, to taste

1. Combine the vinegar, soy sauce, chopped mint, ginger, orange zest, and oil in a bowl.
2. Set the lettuce leaves on a counter. Divide the beef, bean sprouts, cucumber, and mint leaves among the lettuce leaves, then fold in the sides of the lettuce leaves and roll up. Serve 2 rolls per person, with the dipping sauce on the side.

Per serving: 136 Cal, 5 g Fat, 2 g Sat Fat, 46 mg Chol, 192 mg Sod, 4 g Carb, 1 g Fib, 18 g Prot, 24 mg Calc. *POINTS: 3.*

Hummus Pitas

MAKES 2 SERVINGS

Tahini, the paste made from ground sesame seeds, is an ingredient in hummus and other Middle Eastern dishes. If you don't have any on hand (its high fat content means it can go rancid quickly), creamy peanut butter is a terrific stand-in.

½ **cup canned chickpeas, rinsed and drained**
1 **tablespoon plain fat-free yogurt**
1 **teaspoon fresh lemon juice**
1 **teaspoon tahini or natural creamy peanut butter**
¼ **teaspoon garlic salt**
⅛ **teaspoon ground cumin**
1 **drop hot red pepper sauce, or to taste**
1 **(6-inch) pita, split**
1 **kirby cucumber, thinly sliced**
1 **plum tomato, thinly sliced**

1. To make the hummus, puree the chickpeas, yogurt, lemon juice, tahini, garlic salt, cumin, and pepper sauce in a food processor.
2. Heat the pita according to package directions. Divide the hummus between the pita halves, then top with the cucumber and tomato.

Per serving: 207 Cal, 5 g Fat, 1 g Sat Fat, 0 mg Chol, 260 mg Sod, 33 g Carb, 5 g Fib, 8 g Prot, 90 mg Calc. *POINTS: 4.*

Lunch on the Run

Want to get out of the fast-food-lunch rut? Tired of over-stuffed deli sandwiches? It only takes a few minutes to put together a delicious, nutritious lunch for home or the office.
• Drizzle some fresh greens with low-fat dressing and wrap in a flour tortilla.
• Stuff a pita with romaine lettuce, mashed chickpeas, and tahini (or creamy peanut butter).
• Keep individual (3-ounce) cans of tuna and packets of low-fat dressing in your desk; all you need to complete your lunch is a handful of fat-free crackers and some baby carrots.
• Stash an unbaked potato and tablespoon or so of shredded cheese in your tote. At the office, zap the potato in the microwave and then sprinkle on the cheese.

Chili Tacos

MAKES 4 SERVINGS

Let the chili simmer as long as you like after adding the tomatoes. It should be thick enough to serve in about 10 minutes, but the flavor will deepen if you cook it 20 minutes longer.

4 teaspoons olive oil

1 green bell pepper, seeded and finely chopped

1 small onion, minced

4 garlic cloves, minced

1 teaspoon canned sliced jalapeño peppers

1 cup canned red kidney beans, rinsed and drained

¼ pound ground beef (10% or less fat)

¼ pound cooked lean pork, shredded

2 teaspoons ground cumin

1 teaspoon dried oregano

Pinch salt

Freshly ground pepper, to taste

1 cup canned diced tomatoes

8 taco shells

2 cups shredded romaine or iceberg lettuce

1 cup salsa

¼ cup fat-free sour cream

2 tablespoons minced cilantro

1. Heat the oil in a nonstick saucepan. Sauté the bell pepper, onion, garlic, and jalapeño until golden, about 7 minutes. Add the beans, beef, pork, cumin, oregano, salt, and ground pepper. Cook until the beef is browned. Stir in the tomatoes, then reduce the heat and simmer, stirring occasionally, until thickened.

2. Fill the taco shells with the chili, then top with the lettuce, salsa, and sour cream. Sprinkle with the cilantro and serve.

Per serving: 399 Cal, 16 g Fat, 4 g Sat Fat, 45 mg Chol, 972 mg Sod, 40 g Carb, 5 g Fiber, 25 g Prot, 140 mg Calc. *POINTS: 9.*

all-in-the-family favorites

Bean Tostadas with
Corn Salsa and Avocado

Bean Tostadas with Corn Salsa and Avocado

MAKES 4 SERVINGS

Tostadas are open-face tacos. They're a great way to use up leftover chicken, fish, or meat as well as potatoes, rice, and vegetables. Fresh salsa, which you can find near the dairy products in most supermarkets, is higher in vitamin C than bottled salsa (it gets cooked out during processing).

4 small (6-inch) corn tortillas
1 (15½-ounce) can pinto or black beans, rinsed and drained
1 cup fresh salsa
1 (8-ounce) can low-sodium corn kernels, drained
¾ cup shredded reduced-fat sharp cheddar cheese
1 cup shredded romaine lettuce
½ avocado, diced
½ cup fat-free sour cream
2 scallions, thinly sliced
2 tablespoons chopped cilantro (optional)

1. Preheat the oven to 450°F. Arrange the tortillas in single layer on a baking sheet and bake until crisp and light brown around the edges, 5–7 minutes.
2. Meanwhile, in a small saucepan, mix the beans and ½ cup of the salsa; cook, stirring as needed and mashing the beans, until heated through, about 5 minutes. In a small bowl, mix the remaining ½ cup of salsa and the corn.
3. Place the tortillas on plates. Spread each with the bean mixture, then top with the cheese, lettuce, corn mixture, avocado, sour cream, scallions, and cilantro (if using).

Per serving: 326 Cal, 6 g Fat, 3 g Sat Fat, 12 mg Chol, 566 mg Sod, 50 g Carb, 11 g Fib, 20 g Prot, 373 mg Calc. **POINTS: 5.**

cooking flash

Here's an easy way to dice an avocado: Cut it in half lengthwise by running a knife through the center, around the pit. Twist the halves to release one half from the pit. Place that half flat-side down on a cutting board and peel off the skin. Cut the avocado into bite-size cubes. To shred lettuce, stack a few leaves, then roll up and slice crosswise into thin shreds.

Twice-Baked Bacon-Cheddar Potatoes

MAKES 4 SERVINGS

Besides bacon and cheddar, stuff your spuds with low-fat vegetarian chili, pureed cottage cheese, and chives, or sautéed mushrooms with shredded Gruyère cheese.

2 **large baking potatoes, scrubbed**
¼ **cup low-sodium chicken broth**
2 **slices bacon, crisp-cooked and crumbled**
½ **cup shredded reduced-fat sharp cheddar cheese**

1. Preheat the broiler; cover the broiler rack with foil. Prick the potatoes a few times with a fork; place on a paper towel in the microwave. Cook on High until soft, about 8 minutes, turning over after 4 minutes. Let cool 5 minutes. Halve the potatoes lengthwise and scoop the potato flesh into a medium bowl, leaving a ¼-inch shell.
2. Stir the broth into the potato flesh; divide between the potato shells and top with the bacon, then the cheese. Place on the broiler rack and broil until the cheese melts, about 5 minutes.

Per serving: 160 Cal, 4 g Fat, 2 g Sat Fat, 13 mg Chol, 165 mg Sod, 24 g Carb, 2 g Fib, 7 g Prot, 136 mg Calc.
POINTS: 3.

cooking flash

Sautéed cherry tomatoes make a tasty accompaniment to this light dinner. Look for small tomatoes, and leave them whole—they won't take more than 3 minutes to heat through, and their flavor is wonderfully intense and juicy.

Southern Barbecue Sloppy Joes

MAKES 6 SERVINGS

Who doesn't like sloppy joes? Take this quick favorite beyond the realm of the sandwich: It makes a great pasta sauce; or turn it into a chili by adding a can of red kidney beans, then top the chili with chopped onion and fat-free sour cream.

1 tablespoon canola oil
2 onions, chopped
1 green bell pepper, seeded
   and chopped
2 garlic cloves, minced
½ tablespoon ground cumin
1 teaspoon chili powder
1 pound ground skinless turkey breast
1 cup ketchup
2 tablespoons packed dark brown sugar
2 tablespoons Worcestershire sauce
½ teaspoon salt
6 hamburger rolls, split

In a large nonstick skillet, heat the oil. Sauté the onions, pepper, and garlic until softened, about 5 minutes. Stir in the cumin and chili powder; when the vegetables are coated with the spices, stir in the turkey; cook, breaking apart the meat with a wooden spoon, 3 minutes. Add the ketchup, brown sugar, Worcestershire sauce, and salt; cook until the sauce is slightly thickened and the turkey is cooked through, 4–5 minutes. Toast the rolls, if desired, and top with the turkey mixture.

Per serving: 319 Cal, 6 g Fat, 1 g Sat Fat, 47 mg Chol, 1,009 mg Sod, 43 g Carb, 3 g Fib, 25 g Prot, 81 mg Calc. *POINTS: 6.*

Huevos Rancheros

MAKES 4 SERVINGS

Although many people would translate this as Ranchers' Eggs, it is more accurate to call the dish Country-Style Eggs. If you prefer, serve the eggs on the tortillas, and top with the salsa.

2 **tomatoes, chopped**
1 **cup canned black beans,**
   rinsed and drained
1 **small red onion, minced**
½ **cup thawed frozen corn kernels**
½ **cup minced cilantro**
1 **jalapeño pepper, seeded,**
   deveined, and minced
   (wear gloves to prevent irritation)
½ **teaspoon salt**
4 **large eggs**
4 **(6-inch) flour tortillas, heated**

1. To make the salsa, combine the tomatoes, beans, onion, corn, cilantro, jalapeño, and salt in a nonstick skillet. Bring to a boil, then reduce the heat and simmer until the flavors are blended, about 10 minutes.

2. While the salsa is simmering, poach the eggs in another skillet.

3. Divide the salsa among 4 plates, then top each portion with an egg. Serve with the tortillas on the side.

Per serving: 314 Cal, 9 g Fat, 2 g Sat Fat, 213 mg Chol, 921 mg Sod, 45 g Carb, 5 g Fib, 16 g Prot, 58 mg Calc. *POINTS: 6.*

Polenta with Sautéed Mushrooms

MAKES 4 SERVINGS

Smoked mozzarella adds richness to the polenta, and its sharpness contrasts with the mushrooms. If you can't find it, try another smoked cheese like Jarlsberg or Gouda.

4 cups low-sodium vegetable
   or chicken broth
1½ cups stone-ground cornmeal
   ½ teaspoon salt
   1 cup shredded smoked part-skim
      mozzarella cheese
Freshly ground pepper, to taste
   1 tablespoon olive oil
   6 ounces sliced mixed mushrooms
   1 onion, chopped

1. In a 2-quart microwavable bowl, mix the broth, cornmeal, and salt with 2 cups water. Cover with wax paper; cook on High until the cornmeal begins to thicken, about 7 minutes; whisk until smooth. Cook on High until all the liquid is absorbed, about 5 minutes longer. Add the cheese and pepper; stir until the cheese melts into the cornmeal mixture.

2. Meanwhile, in a large nonstick skillet, heat the oil. Sauté the mushrooms and onion until tender, about 8 minutes. Serve the polenta topped with the vegetables.

Per serving: 337 Cal, 11 g Fat, 4 g Sat Fat, 21 mg Chol, 535 mg Sod, 46 g Carb, 5 g Fib, 16 g Prot, 211 mg Calc. ***POINTS: 7.***

shopping flash

Look for packages of already-cleaned-and-sliced exotic mushroom blends—we like shiitake, cremini, and portobello—in the produce aisle.

Sausage and White Bean Stew

MAKES 6 SERVINGS

With this hearty stew, chock-full of sausage and beans as well as green and red vegetables, a chunk of bread is almost superfluous. But you'll want one to sop up the savory juices. For a milder alternative to the broccoli rabe, you can substitute kale or spinach.

1 tablespoon olive oil
½ pound Italian-style turkey sausage, casings removed
1 red onion, chopped
3 garlic cloves, minced
1 teaspoon dried basil leaves, crumbled
½ teaspoon salt
¼ teaspoon freshly ground pepper
1 bunch broccoli rabe, cleaned and coarsely chopped
1 (28-ounce) can crushed tomatoes
1 (15-ounce) can cannellini beans, rinsed and drained
2 tablespoons grated Parmesan cheese

In a large nonstick skillet, heat the oil. Crumble the sausage into the skillet and cook, breaking apart with a wooden spoon, until browned, about 8 minutes. Add the onion, garlic, basil, salt, and pepper; cook, stirring as needed, until fragrant, about 2 minutes. Stir in the broccoli rabe, tomatoes, and beans; cook until the broccoli rabe is wilted, about 5 minutes. Top with the cheese and serve.

Per serving: 201 Cal, 8 g Fat, 2 g Sat Fat, 31 mg Chol, 831 mg Sod, 21 g Carb, 5 g Fib, 14 g Prot, 112 mg Calc. *POINTS: 4.*

Healthy Fast-Food Fixes

• **Pizza night?** Request less cheese and more veggies. Ask your pizzeria if they can substitute part-skim mozzarella for the full-fat variety and whole-wheat crust for regular (if available).

• **Hamburgers on the menu?** They don't have to be ordered deluxe—loaded with cheese and all the extras. Instead, opt for a small plain hamburger with a side salad.

• **Taking out rotisserie chicken?** Stick to white meat and remove the skin before eating. Good sides include a (plain) baked potato or rice pilaf, and a tossed salad.

• **Craving Mexican?** Go for grilled rather than fried entrées. Use plenty of salsa or chili sauce as condiments and skip the sour cream and guacamole.

• **Ordering Chinese?** Fill up on hot-and-sour or wonton soup. Stick with "un-fried" appetizers like steamed vegetable dumplings. Good main dish choices are Moo Shu Vegetables—ask for the filling steamed instead of sautéed—and steamed vegetables with garlic or black bean sauce (served on the side). For a nutritional boost, request brown rice.

Individual Chicken-and-Two-Cheese Pizzas

MAKES 4 SERVINGS

If you're concerned about placing the loaded pizza crusts directly on the oven rack, by all means place them on a baking sheet before topping them with the chicken. Line the baking sheet with foil for easy cleanup. Serve this pizza with a mixed green salad.

2 cups diced cooked skinless chicken
½ cup garlic-herb flavored tomato sauce
1 scallion, thinly sliced
4 small (6-inch) prebaked pizza crust
shells or onion pitas
½ cup shredded reduced-fat
cheddar cheese
½ cup shredded part-skim
mozzarella cheese

Preheat the oven to 500°F. In a medium bowl, mix the chicken, tomato sauce, and scallion. Spoon the mixture evenly onto the pizza crusts; sprinkle with the cheddar and mozzarella. Bake until the cheeses melt and the chicken is heated through, about 10 minutes.

Per serving: 404 Cal, 12 g Fat, 5 g Sat Fat, 78 mg Chol, 706 mg Sod, 38 g Carb, 1 g Fib, 35 g Prot, 311 mg Calc. **POINTS: 9.**

shopping flash

Pick up a precooked chicken in the deli section of your supermarket over the weekend so you'll have leftovers to use during the week. Don't worry if the chicken is flavored; in fact, if you buy a barbecued chicken, use barbecue sauce instead of the tomato sauce.

Cheddar Chicken with Warm Black Bean Salsa

MAKES 4 SERVINGS

This dish is inspired by chicken enchiladas, but it's much less labor-intensive. If you prefer, serve it with quick-cooking brown rice instead of the tortillas.

4 (3-ounce) thin-sliced skinless chicken breasts (¼-inch thick)

½ teaspoon dried oregano, crumbled

¼ teaspoon salt

⅛ teaspoon freshly ground pepper

¾ cup shredded reduced-fat sharp cheddar cheese

1 (14½-ounce) can Mexican-style stewed tomatoes

1 (15-ounce) can black beans, rinsed and drained

2 tablespoons chopped cilantro (optional)

1. Spray a large nonstick skillet with nonstick cooking spray; heat. Sauté the chicken until lightly browned, about 3 minutes; then sprinkle with the oregano, salt, and pepper. Turn over and sauté until cooked through, about 3 minutes longer. Sprinkle the chicken with all but 1 tablespoon of the cheese.

2. Meanwhile, in a small saucepan, bring the tomatoes and beans to a boil. Top the chicken with the black bean salsa, the remaining cheese, and the cilantro (if using) and serve.

Per serving: 287 Cal, 6 g Fat, 3 g Sat Fat, 62 mg Chol, 911 mg Sod, 25 g Carb, 8 g Fib, 35 g Prot, 297 mg Calc. **POINTS: 5.**

shopping flash

If you can't find Mexican-style stewed tomatoes, use plain stewed tomatoes and add a dash of hot red pepper sauce or a spoonful of chopped green chiles—or just use a jar of your favorite salsa. The sharpest cheddar you can find will give the most flavor.

**Cheddar Chicken with
Warm Black Bean Salsa**

Crunchy Tex-Mex Chicken Fingers

MAKES 4 SERVINGS

The crunchy texture of wheat germ makes it a perfect replacement for the breading traditionally used for fried foods. The tender is the strip of meat that connects the chicken breast to the bone. Instead of buying chicken tenders (they can be rather pricey), cut chicken breasts into strips. Compliment these tasty kid favorites with a black bean–corn salad.

1 cup wheat germ
2 teaspoons chili powder
1 teaspoon ground cumin
1 teaspoon garlic powder
½ teaspoon salt
¼ teaspoon cayenne pepper
2 egg whites
1 pound skinless chicken tenders

1. Preheat the oven to 425°F. Spray a baking sheet with nonstick cooking spray.
2. In a shallow dish, mix the wheat germ, chili powder, cumin, garlic powder, salt, and cayenne. In another shallow dish, whisk the egg whites with 2 tablespoons water.
3. Dip the chicken into the egg white mixture, then into the wheat germ mixture. Dip and coat the chicken again in the remaining egg white and wheat germ mixtures. Transfer to the baking sheet. Bake until the chicken is cooked through, about 10 minutes.

Per serving: 270 Cal, 7 g Fat, 1 g Sat Fat, 73 mg Chol, 374 mg Sod, 16 g Carb, 5 g Fib, 37 g Prot, 45 mg Calc.
POINTS: 5.

cooking flash

To make the side salad suggested above, drain and rinse a 15-ounce can of black beans; mix with 1 cup thawed frozen corn kernels and some salsa. Spritz in a little lime juice, if you like.

Chicken with Apricots

MAKES 4 SERVINGS

Kids love this easy entrée—and what's not to love? It has chunks of chicken and dried apricots simmered in a sweet-and-sour sauce. Try this served over orange rice, made by replacing one third of the water with orange juice when you cook the rice.

2 teaspoons peanut oil
2 scallions, thinly sliced (keep white and green parts separate)
1 pound skinless boneless chicken breasts, diced
¼ cup chicken stock (or broth)
3 tablespoons rice-wine vinegar
3 tablespoons ketchup
2 tablespoons sugar
1 cup chopped dried apricots
1 teaspoon cornstarch, dissolved in 1 tablespoon water

1. In a large nonstick skillet, heat the oil. Sauté the white scallion bulbs until softened, about 3 minutes. Add the chicken and sauté until browned, 2–3 minutes.
2. Meanwhile, in a small bowl, combine the stock, vinegar, ketchup, and sugar. Add to the chicken mixture; stir in the apricots. Cover and simmer until the chicken is cooked through, 3–5 minutes. Stir in the dissolved cornstarch; cook until the sauce thickens. Sprinkle with the green scallion tops and serve.

Per serving: 292 Cal, 4 g Fat, 1 g Sat Fat, 66 mg Chol, 252 mg Sod, 35 g Carb, 2 g Fib, 28 g Prot, 37 mg Calc. **POINTS: 6.**

**Maple-Glazed
Chicken with Apples**

Maple-Glazed Chicken with Apples

MAKES 4 SERVINGS

We like the heart-shaped Gala apple for this recipe because it has a crisp sweet taste. Look for its distinctive yellow-orange skin with red stripes in supermarkets and at farmers' markets. If you can't find it, use another firm apple like Golden Delicious or Granny Smith.

1 cup apple cider or juice

1 firm apple, cored and cut into 8 wedges

⅓ cup maple syrup

½ teaspoon dried thyme leaves, crumbled

4 (4-ounce) thin-sliced skinless chicken breasts (¼-inch thick)

1. Line the broiler rack with foil; preheat the broiler. In a medium nonstick saucepan, mix the apple cider, apple, maple syrup and thyme; bring to a boil over medium–high heat. Cook until the apple is tender and the sauce is reduced by half, about 8 minutes. Remove from the heat and keep warm.

2. Place the chicken on the broiler rack and brush on both sides with half of the maple mixture; broil 4 inches from the heat until lightly browned, about 3 minutes. Turn and brush the top with the remaining maple mixture; broil until the chicken is cooked through, about 3 minutes longer. Serve with the apple wedges on the side.

Per serving: 267 Cal, 2 g Fat, 1 g Sat Fat, 69 mg Chol, 190 mg Sod, 34 g Carb, 2 g Fib, 28 g Prot, 49 mg Calc. *POINTS: 5.*

cooking flash

When cooking firm apples, leave the peels on. It saves time, boosts nutrients and fiber, and helps the apples keep their shape.

Turkey-Mushroom Shepherd's Pie

MAKES 6 SERVINGS

Craving comfort food? This hearty dish will fill you up without slowing you down. It's also tasty made with extra-lean ground beef. If green beans aren't in season, thaw two 8-ounce boxes of frozen cut green beans to use instead, or use the same amount of green peas.

1½ **pounds red potatoes, scrubbed and diced**
¾ **cup fat-free milk**
½ **teaspoon salt**
¼ **teaspoon freshly ground pepper**
1 **teaspoon olive oil**
2 **garlic cloves, minced**
1 **carrot, chopped**
1 **onion, chopped**
½ **pound cremini or white mushrooms, chopped**
1 **pound ground skinless turkey breast**
¼ **teaspoon dried thyme leaves, crumbled**
2½ **tablespoons all-purpose flour**
1 **cup fat-free chicken broth**
½ **pound green beans, trimmed, chopped, and lightly steamed**

1. Preheat the oven to 400°F. Place the potatoes in a medium saucepan and add cold water to cover; bring to a boil. Reduce the heat and simmer until fork-tender, 10–12 minutes. Drain well, then mash with the milk, salt, and pepper.

2. Meanwhile, heat a large nonstick skillet; swirl in the oil. Sauté the garlic, carrot, onion, and mushrooms until they begin to soften, about 5 minutes. Add the turkey and thyme; cook, breaking apart the meat with a wooden spoon, until no longer pink, 5–8 minutes. Stir in the flour; cook, stirring, 2 minutes. Stir in the broth; cook until thickened, about 2 minutes.

3. Transfer the turkey and vegetables to a shallow 2–3 quart casserole. Top with the beans, then spread on the potatoes. Bake until the potatoes are heated through, about 5 minutes.

Per serving: 275 Cal, 7 g Fat, 2 g Sat Fat, 60 mg Chol, 338 mg Sod, 32 g Carb, 5 g Fib, 21 g Prot, 83 mg Calc. *POINTS: 5.*

Sweet-and-Sour Pork

MAKES 4 SERVINGS

The sweet-tart pineapple and tangy Asian flavors are the perfect complement to succulent pork. Some supermarkets sell lean pork loin cut into cubes; if yours is one, buying it precut will save a little prep time.

1 tablespoon olive oil

2 tablespoons hoisin sauce

2 teaspoons packed brown sugar

1 teaspoon soy sauce

¼ teaspoon ground ginger

½ pound boneless lean pork loin, cubed

1 red bell pepper, seeded and cut into 1-inch pieces

3 scallions, sliced

1 cup drained canned unsweetened pineapple chunks (reserve 1 tablespoon juice)

1. In a large nonstick skillet or wok, heat the oil. In a gallon-size sealable plastic bag, mix the hoisin sauce, brown sugar, soy sauce, and ginger; add the pork. Seal the bag, squeezing out the air; turn to coat the pork. Let the bagged pork stand while you cook the vegetables.

2. In the skillet, stir-fry the bell pepper and scallions until softened, about 5 minutes. Transfer to a plate.

3. Transfer the pork to the skillet, reserving the marinade; stir-fry the pork until browned, about 2–3 minutes. Add the marinade, pineapple, and pineapple juice; stir-fry until the pork is cooked through, about 5 minutes longer. Return the vegetables to the skillet and heat to serving temperature, about 2 minutes.

Per serving: 166 Cal, 7 g Fat, 2 g Sat Fat, 31 mg Chol, 243 mg Sod, 13 g Carb, 1 g Fib, 13 g Prot, 26 mg Calc. ***POINTS: 4.***

cooking flash

Rice is the obvious side dish for this zesty recipe. However, if you don't like the texture of quick-cooking rice, make a big batch of regular rice when you have time; refrigerate it to use within a week, or freeze it for up to 3 months. Since rice hardens when chilled, add 2 tablespoons of water for each cup of rice when you reheat it.

Pork Chops with Sweet Potatoes and Pears

MAKES 4 SERVINGS

Pork's richness marries well with sweet and fruity accompaniments. You could use pineapple chunks or apricots in place of the pears, or substitute leftover winter squash for the yams.

- 1 **tablespoon vegetable oil**
- 1 **tablespoon all-purpose flour**
- 1 **teaspoon curry powder**
- ¾ **teaspoon salt**
- 4 **(4-ounce) boneless center-cut pork loin chops**
- 1 **(15-ounce) can yams in light syrup, drained**
- 1 **(15-ounce) can pear slices in pear juice, drained (reserve ½ cup juice)**
- ½ **teaspoon dried thyme leaves, crumbled**
- ⅛ **teaspoon freshly ground pepper**

1. In a large nonstick skillet, heat the oil. In a large sealable plastic bag, mix the flour, curry powder, and ¼ teaspoon of the salt. Add the pork and shake to coat.

2. Transfer the pork to the skillet; sauté until cooked through, about 3 minutes on each side.

3. Meanwhile, cut the yams into bite-size chunks; add to the pork with the pears, reserved pear juice, thyme, pepper, and the remaining ½ teaspoon of salt. Reduce the heat and simmer, covered, about 5 minutes; uncover and simmer until the pork is cooked through, about 2 minutes longer.

Per serving: 372 Cal, 11 g Fat, 3 g Sat Fat, 92 mg Chol, 540 mg Sod, 34 g Carb, 4 g Fib, 33 g Prot, 36 mg Calc. ***POINTS: 8.***

cooking flash

We used bone-in pork chops in the photograph, but you can choose boneless pork chops for speedier cooking. Although bone-in cuts of meat tend to have more flavor and stay juicier during cooking, bone takes much longer to heat than muscle, so boneless cuts cook much faster.

**Pork Chops with
Sweet Potatoes and Pears**

Stovetop Veal Parmesan

MAKES 4 SERVINGS

To keep it lean, we've skipped the traditional egg-and-bread coating for the cutlets—dredging them in seasoned flour adds plenty of flavor. You can substitute turkey or chicken cutlets for the veal, if you like.

1 tablespoon all-purpose flour

¼ teaspoon salt

4 (3-ounce) thin-sliced veal cutlets (⅛-inch thick)

2 cups marinara sauce

¾ cup shredded part-skim mozzarella cheese

2 tablespoons grated Parmesan cheese

⅛ teaspoon freshly ground pepper

1. Spray a very large (12-inch) nonstick skillet with nonstick cooking spray; heat. Meanwhile, on a sheet of wax paper or a plate, mix the flour and salt. Lightly dredge the veal in the flour.

2. Transfer the veal to the skillet; sauté until golden brown, about 3 minutes; turn over and sauté 1–2 minutes longer.

3. Pour the marinara sauce around the veal, then sprinkle the cutlets with the mozzarella and Parmesan. Reduce the heat and simmer, covered, until the cheeses melt, the sauce is bubbling, and the cutlets are cooked through, 3–5 minutes. Sprinkle with the pepper and serve.

Per serving: 268 Cal, 12 g Fat, 4 g Sat Fat, 83 mg Chol, 1,036 mg Sod, 15 g Carb, 3 g Fib, 26 g Prot, 227 mg Calc. *POINTS: 6.*

cooking flash

If your supermarket doesn't carry veal cutlets (sometimes marketed as scaloppine) that are superthin, place regular cutlets between two sheets of wax paper and pound them gently to ⅛-inch thickness with a meat mallet or a small heavy skillet.

Peanut-Flavored Ginger Beef with Vegetables

MAKES 4 SERVINGS

You can substitute other vegetables, such as bell peppers and scallions, for the carrots and broccoli in this dish. To cut down on prep time, start off with presliced meat and ready-cut vegetables from the supermarket. Then enjoy this Asian stir-fry served over quick-cooking rice.

1 tablespoon reduced-sodium soy sauce

1 tablespoon creamy peanut butter

¼ teaspoon crushed red pepper flakes (optional)

3 teaspoons vegetable oil

¾ pound boneless top round steak, cut into strips

2 tablespoons grated peeled fresh gingerroot (or ½ teaspoon ground ginger)

2 cups baby carrots, halved lengthwise, or precut carrot sticks

2 cups broccoli florets

2 garlic cloves, thinly sliced

2 tablespoons chopped cilantro (optional)

1. In a small bowl, mix the soy sauce, peanut butter, pepper flakes (if using), and ¼ cup water; set aside.

2. Place a very large nonstick skillet or wok with a lid over high heat until a drop of water skitters. Heat 2 teaspoons of the oil until it shimmers. Stir-fry the steak until lightly browned, about 2 minutes. Add the gingerroot and cook, stirring, 2 minutes longer. Transfer to a bowl and keep warm.

3. In the skillet, heat the remaining teaspoon of oil. Stir-fry the carrots 1 minute; add broccoli and garlic; stir-fry 1 minute longer. Add 1–2 tablespoons water; simmer, covered, until the vegetables are tender-crisp, about 1 minute. Return the steak and gingerroot to the skillet; add the peanut butter mixture and stir-fry until heated through, about 1 minute. Remove from the heat; stir in cilantro (if using) and serve.

Per serving: 311 Cal, 11 g Fat, 3 g Sat Fat, 71 mg Chol, 293 mg Sod, 22 g Carb, 5 g Fib, 33 g Prot, 103 mg Calc. *POINTS: 6.*

Chili-Beef Quesadillas

MAKES 4 SERVINGS

A quesadilla is the Mexican version of a grilled cheese sandwich: Cheese and other ingredients like meat, beans, or veggies are layered between flour tortillas and are then fried or baked. Quesadillas are often served as appetizers as well as light entrées.

½ **pound lean (10% or less fat)
    ground beef**
1 **small onion, diced**
1 **garlic clove, minced**
1 **(4-ounce) can diced green chiles,
    drained**
1 **tablespoon chili powder**
¼ **teaspoon salt**
4 **medium (8-inch) fat-free flour tortillas**
¾ **cup shredded reduced-fat
    cheddar cheese**
½ **cup fat-free sour cream**
1 **large tomato, diced**
2 **tablespoons chopped cilantro**

1. Preheat the oven to 400°F. In a large nonstick skillet, cook the beef, onion, and garlic, breaking apart the beef with a wooden spoon, until it is no longer pink, 3–5 minutes. Stir in the chiles, chili powder, salt, and ¼ cup water; cook, stirring occasionally, until the liquid evaporates, about 10 minutes.

2. Place 2 of the tortillas on a baking sheet; top with the beef mixture, then sprinkle evenly with the cheese. Top with the remaining 2 tortillas, pressing lightly. Bake until the cheese melts, about 8 minutes. Let stand 5 minutes. Cut each quesadilla in half, then cut each half into 3 wedges. Top with the sour cream, tomato, and cilantro and serve.

Per serving: 388 Cal, 13 g Fat, 5 g Sat Fat, 33 mg Chol, 557 mg Sod, 41 g Carb, 3 g Fib, 27 g Prot, 286 mg Calc. *POINTS: 8.*

cooking flash

Quesadillas can be made on the stove, but they can be tricky to turn. If you go this route, heat one tortilla in a large skillet, then cover half of it with the beef and cheese; fold the other half over and press lightly. Turn the quesadilla after a minute or so, lifting from the round edge to prevent spilling the filling. When the tortilla is lightly browned and the cheese is melted, cut into 3 wedges.

Easy Asian Swordfish Kebabs

MAKES 4 SERVINGS

If you have the time, boost the flavor of the swordfish by marinating it in the refrigerator for 2 to 8 hours, turning the bag occasionally. Round out this kebab meal with soba noodles and steamed sugar-snap peas.

3 **tablespoons teriyaki sauce**
2 **tablespoons hoisin sauce**
2 **teaspoons grated peeled gingerroot**
2 **garlic cloves, minced**
¼ **teaspoon crushed red pepper flakes**
1 **pound swordfish steak, cut**
   into chunks

1. In a gallon-size sealable plastic bag, mix the teriyaki sauce, hoisin sauce, gingerroot, garlic, and pepper flakes with ¼ cup water. Pour half of the marinade into a small saucepan; add the swordfish to the bag. Seal the bag, squeezing out air; turn to coat the fish.

2. Spray the broiler rack with nonstick cooking spray; preheat the broiler. Thread the swordfish onto 4 (12-inch) metal skewers; place the kebabs on the rack. Drain the remaining marinade into the saucepan.

3. Bring the marinade to a boil and boil, stirring constantly, 3 minutes. Broil the kebabs, turning frequently and brushing with the marinade, until the swordfish is browned on the outside and just opaque inside, 5–8 minutes.

Per serving: 179 Cal, 6 g Fat, 2 g Sat Fat, 51 mg Chol, 302 mg Sod, 5 g Carb, 0 g Fib, 25 g Prot, 11 mg Calc.
POINTS: 4.

everybody loves pasta (grains, too!)

Cavatappi with Olive-Caper Sauce

Cavatappi with Olive-Caper Sauce

MAKES 4 SERVINGS

This piquant sauce of capers, olives, and sun-dried tomatoes is easy to put together. Cavatappi are thick ridged pasta spirals. The sauce works equally well with fusilli, radiatore, rotelle, or small shells, if you prefer.

10 **sun-dried tomato halves (not packed in oil)**
2 **teaspoons olive oil**
1 **red onion, chopped**
20 **small kalamata or gaeta olives, pitted and chopped**
¼ **cup chopped basil**
1 **teaspoon dried marjoram**
Freshly ground pepper, to taste
1 **cup low-sodium vegetable broth**
2 **tablespoons dry white wine**
1 **tablespoon capers, drained and minced**
2 **cups cavatappi**

1. Soak the sun-dried tomatoes in warm water to cover until soft, about 15 minutes. Drain and pat dry with paper towels, then chop them.

2. Heat the oil in a nonstick skillet, then add the tomatoes, onion, olives, basil, marjoram, and pepper. Sauté until the onion is tender, then stir in the broth, wine, and capers. Bring to a boil, then reduce the heat and simmer until slightly thickened, about 10 minutes.

3. Meanwhile, cook the cavatappi according to package directions. Drain and put in a serving bowl. Top with the sauce and toss to coat.

Per serving: 291 Cal, 6 g Fat, 1 g Sat Fat, 1 mg Chol, 400 mg Sod, 51 g Carb, 9 g Prot, 5 g Fib, 58 mg Calc. **POINTS: 6.**

cooking flash

You can buy olives that are pitted, but they're most often canned, so their flavor and texture are less than ideal. To pit a lot of olives, put them in a plastic bag and press on them with the bottom of a skillet; to pit a few, just set them on a cutting board and press with the flat side of a chef's knife.

Spaghetti with Fresh Tomatoes and Basil

MAKES 4 SERVINGS

Nothing says summer as much as fresh-picked tomatoes and basil still warm from the sun. This sauce is not cooked; the heat from the pasta brings forth the flavors of the vegetables, so use the freshest vine-ripened tomatoes you can find.

8 ripe plum tomatoes, chopped
4 teaspoons extra-virgin olive oil
1 garlic clove, bruised
¼ teaspoon salt
Freshly ground pepper, to taste
6 ounces spaghetti
½ cup minced basil

1. Combine the tomatoes, oil, garlic, salt, and pepper in a serving bowl.
2. Cook the spaghetti according to package directions. When it is almost done, remove the garlic from the tomato mixture and discard. Drain the spaghetti and add to the tomato mixture; toss gently to coat. Sprinkle with the basil.

Per serving: 215 Cal, 6 g Fat, 1 g Sat Fat, 0 mg Chol, 144 mg Sod, 36 g Carb, 2 g Fib, 6 g Prot, 60 mg Calc. *POINTS: 4.*

Linguine with Herbed Butter

MAKES 4 SERVINGS

Try this recipe and see whether you don't agree that a small amount of butter is the perfect carrier for herbs. If you're preparing a meal for hearty eaters, serve this with Mediterranean Shrimp [page 154].

6 ounces linguine
2 tablespoons unsalted butter
2 tablespoons minced parsley
1 tablespoon minced basil
1 tablespoon thyme leaves
1 tablespoon minced oregano
1 garlic clove, bruised and peeled
¼ teaspoon salt
Freshly ground pepper, to taste

1. Cook the linguine according to package directions. Drain and put in a serving bowl.
2. Meanwhile, melt the butter in a small nonstick skillet. Add the parsley, basil, thyme, oregano, garlic, salt, and pepper. Reduce the heat and cook until the herbs wilt. Discard the garlic. Pour the herbed butter over the linguine and toss to coat. Serve immediately.

Per serving: 218 Cal, 7 g Fat, 4 g Sat Fat, 16 mg Chol, 151 mg Sod, 30 g Carb, 2 g Fib, 10 g Prot, 50 mg Calc. ***POINTS: 5.***

Linguine Verde

MAKES 4 SERVINGS

This is a perfect dish for summer, using fresh-from-the-garden ingredients in an uncooked sauce. The heat of the pasta helps to wilt the greens and herbs.

½ **pound linguine**
1 **bunch arugula, cleaned and torn (about 3 cups)**
1 **bunch watercress, cleaned and torn (about 2 cups)**
2 **tomatoes, peeled, seeded, and cut into strips**
½ **cup firmly packed torn basil**
4–5 **mint leaves, chopped**
4 **teaspoons extra-virgin olive oil**
¼ **teaspoon salt**
2 **tablespoons grated pecorino Romano cheese**
¼ **cup grated Parmesan cheese**
Freshly ground pepper, to taste

1. Cook the linguine according to package directions.
2. Meanwhile, combine the arugula, watercress, tomatoes, basil, and mint in a serving bowl. Sprinkle with the oil and salt; toss to combine. Drain the linguine and add to the greens, then sprinkle with the Romano, half of the Parmesan, and the pepper. Toss to coat, sprinkle with the remaining Parmesan, and serve.

Per serving: 319 Cal, 12 g Fat, 5 g Sat Fat, 17 mg Chol, 532 mg Sod, 40 g Carb, 4 g Fib, 14 g Prot, 367 mg Calc. *POINTS: 7.*

cooking flash

For a milder flavor, replace some of the arugula and watercress with escarole, parsley, or spinach.

Linguine Verde

Fettuccine with Roasted Vegetable Sauce

 MAKES 4 SERVINGS

Roasting vegetables heightens their natural sweetness and imparts a delectable smoky flavor. This just might become your favorite sauce.

1 **red bell pepper, seeded and cut into ½-inch slices**
½ **tomato, seeded and chopped**
½ **onion, chopped**
2 **teaspoons olive oil**
½ **teaspoon salt**
Freshly ground pepper, to taste
½ **cup water**
2 **tablespoons vegetable broth**
2 **tablespoons Neufchâtel cheese**
6 **ounces fettuccine**
4 **teaspoons grated Parmesan cheese**

1. Preheat the oven to 425°F. Combine the bell pepper, tomato, onion, oil, salt, pepper, and water in a roasting pan. Roast the vegetables, tossing occasionally, until tender, about 15 minutes. Transfer to a food processor or blender, add the broth and Neufchâtel, and puree.

2. Meanwhile, cook the fettuccine according to package directions. Drain and put in a serving bowl. Top with the sauce and toss to coat. Sprinkle with the Parmesan and serve.

Per serving: 214 Cal, 4 g Fat, 1 g Sat Fat, 3 mg Chol, 123 mg Sod, 36 g Carb, 2 g Fib, 8 g Prot, 44 mg Calc.
POINTS: 4.

Easy Ziti

MAKES 6 SERVINGS

The ultimate express-lane dinner! To make variations of this basic dish, use pasta shapes such as penne or shells, or stir in 1½ cups sautéed chopped mushrooms, zucchini, or a 10-ounce box of thawed frozen peas when you mix the pasta and sauce.

1 (16-ounce) jar reduced-fat spaghetti sauce
½ cup part-skim ricotta cheese
1 (1-pound) box ziti
½ cup shredded reduced-fat Italian cheese blend

1. Preheat the broiler. In a large bowl, mix the spaghetti sauce and ricotta thoroughly, until smooth.

2. Meanwhile, cook the ziti according to package directions. Drain and stir into the sauce, then spread into a 9 x 13-inch metal baking dish. Sprinkle with the cheese blend. Broil until the cheese is melted and golden, about 5 minutes.

Per serving: 353 Cal, 4 g Fat, 2 g Sat Fat, 8 mg Chol, 326 mg Sod, 64 g Carb, 3 g Fib, 16 g Prot, 146 mg Calc. **POINTS: 7.**

7 Steps to Perfect Pasta

1. Look for dried pasta made of durum wheat—it's a very hard wheat, so the pasta will absorb less water as it cooks and won't become soggy or mushy.

2. Use lots of water—about 1 quart of water for each ¼ pound of dried pasta.

3. Salted water takes longer to come to a boil than does unsalted, so add the salt (for flavor) just before you add the pasta. (Don't add oil, though. It will coat the pasta and keep the sauce from clinging.)

4. Add the pasta to the boiling water and stir. Begin timing when the pasta water comes back to a boil, not from the moment you add the pasta.

5. Heed the cooking time on the pasta box. This will vary by type of pasta (super-skinny capellini will cook in 2 to 3 minutes; a dense shape like radiatore may take close to 15 minutes) and from one brand to the next, depending on the type of flour used.

6. Test at the earlier time in the cooking time range. Take a bite of the pasta: It should be tender but still have a little firmness to it (what Italians call al dente).

7. Pasta will continue to cook after you drain it, so transfer to a colander just a little before you think it's done. After draining, give the colander a few shakes to rid pasta of excess water.

Fettuccine with Creamy Spinach Sauce

MAKES 4 SERVINGS

If you love creamy pasta sauces, remember this recipe—pureed ricotta cheese is a superb alternative to fat-laden heavy cream. To get the smoothest possible texture, puree the cheese in a blender.

6 **ounces fettuccine**
2 **teaspoons olive oil**
3 **shallots, chopped**
1 **garlic clove, minced**
2 **cups chopped cleaned spinach**
1 **cup canned crushed tomatoes**
  (no salt added)
¼ **teaspoon salt**
½ **cup part-skim ricotta cheese, pureed**
¼ **teaspoon freshly ground pepper**

1. Cook the fettuccine according to package directions. Drain, reserving ½ cup of the cooking liquid, and keep warm.
2. Meanwhile, heat the oil in a nonstick saucepan, then add the shallots. Sauté until softened, then add the garlic and cook until fragrant. Stir in the spinach, tomatoes, and salt and cook until the spinach wilts.
3. Add the fettuccine, ¼ cup of the reserved cooking liquid, and the ricotta. Cook, tossing, until heated through. If you like, add more of the cooking liquid to make the sauce creamier. Sprinkle with the pepper and serve.

Per serving: 246 Cal, 6 g Fat, 2 g Sat Fat, 9 mg Chol, 217 mg Sod, 39 g Carb, 3 g Fib, 11 g Prot, 140 mg Calc. ***POINTS: 5.***

Farfalle with Cauliflower and Hot Pepper

 MAKES 4 SERVINGS

Turn humble cauliflower into something wonderful with this southern Italian specialty. The secrets are to cook the anchovies gently—this gets rid of the fishiness—and to avoid overcooking the cauliflower. The cauliflower should be al dente, just like the farfalle.

4 teaspoons olive oil
8 anchovy fillets, rinsed and dried
½ cup low-sodium chicken broth
4 cups farfalle
1 small head cauliflower,
   cut into small florets
¼ cup chopped flat-leaf parsley
¼–½ teaspoon crushed red pepper

1. Heat the oil in a nonstick skillet over low heat. Add the anchovies and cook, stirring gently, until they disintegrate. Add the broth and bring to a boil. Reduce the heat and simmer until the liquid is reduced by half, about 5 minutes. Remove skillet from the heat.

2. Meanwhile, cook the farfalle according to package directions. Drain and put in a serving bowl.

3. Steam the cauliflower until tender, 8–10 minutes. Add to the pasta with the anchovy sauce, parsley, and crushed red pepper; toss to combine and serve.

Per serving: 406 Cal, 8 g Fat, 1 g Sat Fat, 7 mg Chol, 341 mg Sod, 68 g Carb, 8 g Fib, 17 g Prot, 75 mg Calc. *POINTS: 8.*

cooking flash
If you prefer, broccoli, broccoflower, or broccolini would be an ideal substitute for the cauliflower.

Fusilli with Pureed Yellow Pepper Sauce

MAKES 4 SERVINGS

To turn this lovely sauce into a flavorful dip for a crudité platter, substitute 4 ounces light cream cheese for the ricotta.

¾ **cup water**
1 **yellow bell pepper, seeded and chopped**
1 **onion, chopped**
½ **tomato, chopped**
2 **teaspoons olive oil**
¼ **teaspoon salt**
Freshly ground pepper, to taste
2 **cups fusilli**
¼ **cup part-skim ricotta cheese**
2 **tablespoons minced parsley**
4 **teaspoons grated Parmesan cheese**

1. Combine the water, bell pepper, onion, tomato, oil, salt, and ground pepper in a nonstick skillet over medium-low heat. Cover and cook, stirring frequently, until the vegetables are tender and the liquid evaporates, 15–18 minutes; add more water, ¼ cup at a time, if the liquid evaporates too fast.
2. Meanwhile, cook the fusilli according to package directions. Drain and put in a serving bowl.
3. Transfer the vegetables to a blender or food processor; add the ricotta and puree. Pour over the fusilli and toss to coat. Sprinkle with the parsley and Parmesan and serve.

Per serving: 233 Cal, 5 g Fat, 2 g Sat Fat, 6 mg Chol, 199 mg Sod, 38 g Carb, 2 g Fib, 9 g Prot, 90 mg Calc.
POINTS: 5.

shopping flash

If yellow bell peppers are unavailable, red or orange will also work. Steer clear of green peppers, though. Their flavor is too strong for this dish.

Fusilli with
Pureed Yellow
Pepper Sauce

Asian Noodles in Satay Sauce

MAKES 4 SERVINGS

Traditionally made with udon noodles, this tasty dish works just as well with fettuccine, which is more commonly available. Because peanut butter is a primary ingredient in a satay, you just might be able to talk your kids into trying this.

½ **cup water**
3 **carrots, thinly sliced**
1 **cup broccoli florets**
1 **cup thinly sliced mushrooms**
1 **cup snow peas**
3 **scallions, thinly sliced**
1 **tablespoon grated peeled fresh ginger**
3 **garlic cloves, minced**
6 **ounces fettuccine**
¼ **cup peanut butter**
3 **tablespoons reduced-sodium soy sauce**
¼ **cup fresh lime juice**
1 **tablespoon honey**
1 **small red bell pepper, seeded and diced**

1. Bring ¼ cup of the water to a boil in a skillet. Add the carrots, broccoli, and mushrooms, then bring back to a boil. Reduce the heat, cover, and simmer until the vegetables are just tender, about 4 minutes. Add the snow peas, scallions, ginger, and garlic. Cook, uncovered, until the snow peas soften.

2. Meanwhile, cook the fettuccine according to package directions; drain.

3. Combine the peanut butter, soy sauce, lime juice, honey, and the remaining ¼ cup water in a bowl. Stir into the vegetables. Add the bell pepper and the fettuccine; toss to coat and serve.

Per serving: 346 Cal, 10 g Fat, 2 g Sat Fat, 40 mg Chol, 562 mg Sod, 52 g Carb, 6 g Fib, 15 g Prot, 81 mg Calc.
POINTS: 7.

Sweet and Spicy Chicken with Orzo

MAKES 4 SERVINGS

Orzo, a rice-shaped pasta, is a perfect accompaniment to sweet ginger-spiced chicken.

1 **cup orzo**
2 **tablespoons chopped flat-leaf parsley**
4 **teaspoons olive oil**
1 **onion, finely chopped**
4 **garlic cloves, minced**
½ **teaspoon cinnamon**
½ **teaspoon salt**
¼ **teaspoon ground ginger**
¼ **teaspoon cayenne**
2 **(8-ounce) jars tomato sauce (no salt added)**
1 **tablespoon honey**
1 **pound cooked chicken breast strips**

1. Cook the orzo according to package directions. Drain and put in a serving bowl. Mix in the parsley and 2 teaspoons of the oil. Keep warm.

2. Meanwhile, heat the remaining 2 teaspoons oil in a nonstick saucepan, then add the onion, garlic, cinnamon, salt, ginger, and cayenne. Sauté until the onion is soft, then stir in the tomato sauce and honey. Cook, stirring frequently, until the sauce comes to a boil. Add the chicken and heat to serving temperature. Spoon the chicken and sauce over the orzo.

Per serving: 401 Cal, 9 g Fat, 2 g Sat Fat, 72 mg Chol, 359 mg Sod, 47 g Carb, 3 g Fib, 34 g Prot, 52 mg Calc
POINTS: 8.

Pasta with Kale and Sausage

MAKES 4 SERVINGS

Don't use long pasta in this dish. Chunky shapes or tubes like radiatore, campanelle, medium shells, or rigatoni are better. Their nooks and crannies trap the chunks of sausage, which would slide right off longer noodles.

1 **onion, finely chopped**
½ **cup finely chopped seeded green bell pepper**
¾ **pound Italian-style turkey sausage, casings removed**
1 **bunch kale, cleaned and chopped**
⅓ **cup water**
1 **(14½-ounce) can chopped tomatoes**
½ **pound pasta shapes**

1. Spray a nonstick skillet with nonstick spray and set over medium–high heat. Add the onion, bell pepper, and sausage. Sauté, breaking apart the sausage with a spoon, until the vegetables are tender and the sausage is browned. Add the kale in handfuls, stirring as each batch wilts. Add the water, then cook, partially covered, until the kale is tender, about 5 minutes. Stir in the tomatoes and heat the mixture through.

2. Meanwhile, cook the pasta according to package directions. Drain and put in a serving bowl. Add the sauce; toss to combine and serve.

Per serving: 395 Cal, 10 g Fat, 3 g Sat Fat, 64 mg Chol, 766 mg Sod, 53 g Carb, 6 g Fib, 27 g Prot, 209 mg Calc. *POINTS: 8.*

cooking flash

For a vegetarian variation, omit the sausage and stir in a can of cannellini beans with the tomatoes.

Fusilli with Turkey, Arugula, and Plum Tomatoes

MAKES 4 SERVINGS

Fun fusilli pasta, shaped like small spirals, pairs with turkey and fresh plum tomatoes. Arugula, an aromatic, piquant salad green, adds a peppery touch to this festive dish.

2 **bunches arugula, cleaned and coarsely chopped**
6 **plum tomatoes, coarsely chopped**
½ **pound cooked turkey breast, cubed**
⅓ **cup red-wine vinegar**
2 **shallots, minced**
4 **teaspoons olive oil**
2 **garlic cloves, minced**
1 **teaspoon freshly ground pepper**
½ **teaspoon salt**
2 **cups fusilli**

1. Combine the arugula, tomatoes, turkey, vinegar, shallots, oil, garlic, pepper, and salt in a large bowl. Cover and let stand at room temperature.

2. Cook the fusilli according to package directions. Drain and add to the turkey mixture; toss to coat.

Per serving: 310 Cal, 6 g Fat, 1 g Sat Fat, 48 mg Chol, 341 mg Sod, 40 g Carb, 3 g Fib, 24 g Prot, 70 mg Calc. *POINTS: 6.*

cooking flash

For a slightly different flavor, use spinach instead of the arugula and smoked turkey breast instead of regular turkey.

**Capellini with Smoked
Salmon and Caviar**

Capellini with Smoked Salmon and Caviar

MAKES 4 SERVINGS

This elegant entrée is perfect when you're celebrating a special occasion. Serve it with roasted asparagus and a chilled dry white wine like Pinot Grigio.

2 teaspoons olive oil

2 scallions, sliced

¼ cup low-sodium chicken broth

2 tablespoons heavy cream

2 tablespoons vodka

6 ounces capellini

¼ pound smoked salmon, cut into thin strips

1 ounce caviar

1. Heat the oil in a nonstick skillet, then add the scallions. Sauté until they just begin to soften, then reduce the heat and stir in the broth, cream, and vodka. Cook, stirring constantly, until just heated through (do not let the sauce come to a boil).

2. Meanwhile, cook the capellini according to package directions. Drain and put in a serving bowl. Pour the sauce over the capellini and toss to coat. Add the salmon and caviar, then toss to combine.

Per serving: 262 Cal, 8 g Fat, 2 g Sat Fat, 57 mg Chol, 320 mg Sod, 33 g Carb, 1 g Fib, 12 g Prot, 20 mg Calc. *POINTS: 6.*

Cavatelli with Shrimp and Arugula

MAKES 4 SERVINGS

Cavatelli is a shell-shaped pasta with a ruffled edge. If you prefer, you can use medium shells, or even gnocchi.

8 **sun-dried tomato halves (not packed in oil)**
2 **cups cavatelli**
4 **teaspoons olive oil**
3 **garlic cloves, minced**
¼ **teaspoon crushed red pepper**
¾ **pound medium shrimp, peeled and deveined (leave tails on)**
2 **bunches arugula, cleaned and torn**
4 **scallions, thinly sliced**
¼ **teaspoon salt**

1. Soak the sun-dried tomatoes in warm water to cover until soft, about 15 minutes. Drain and pat dry with paper towels, then chop them.

2. Meanwhile, cook the cavatelli according to package directions. Drain, reserving ¼ cup of the cooking liquid, and put in a serving bowl.

3. While the cavatelli cooks, heat the oil in a nonstick skillet, then add the garlic and crushed red pepper. Sauté until fragrant, then add the shrimp; sauté until they turn pink. Add the arugula, scallions, and tomatoes and cook until the arugula wilts. Spoon over the cavatelli and toss to combine. Sprinkle with the reserved cooking liquid and salt, then toss again.

Per serving: 321 Cal, 7 g Fat, 1 g Sat Fat, 129 mg Chol, 295 mg Sod, 39 g Carb, 4 g Fib, 25 g Prot, 137 mg Calc. **POINTS: 6.**

Vegetable Fried Rice

MAKES 4 SERVINGS

Next time you make rice, cook some extra and save it for this recipe. Fried rice is easiest to make when the rice is cold. We like this with plenty of garlic—you may want to omit a clove or two.

3 **eggs**
4 **scallions, sliced**
½ **cup chopped cilantro**
2 **tablespoons reduced-sodium soy sauce**
2 **tablespoons water**
¼ **teaspoon sugar**
2 **teaspoons Asian (dark) sesame oil**
1 **leek, cleaned and cut into thin strips**
1 **carrot, thinly sliced**
1 **red bell pepper, seeded and chopped**
2 **tablespoons grated peeled fresh ginger**
5 **garlic cloves, minced**
3 **cups cold cooked rice**
¼ **cup unsalted dry-roasted peanuts, chopped**
2 **tablespoons rice-wine or cider vinegar**
½ **teaspoon salt**

1. Whisk the eggs, ¼ of the scallions, ¼ of the cilantro, 1 tablespoon soy sauce, the water, and sugar in a bowl, blending until the sugar dissolves.
2. Spray a nonstick skillet with nonstick spray and set over medium heat. Pour in the egg mixture and cook, stirring gently, until scrambled. Remove from the skillet and let cool, then cut into thin strips.
3. Heat the oil in the nonstick skillet, then add the leek, carrot, and bell pepper. Sauté until softened, then add the ginger and garlic and sauté until fragrant. Add the rice and cook, stirring constantly, until heated through. Stir in the peanuts, vinegar, salt, the cooked eggs, and the remaining scallions, cilantro, and soy sauce. Cook, stirring the mixture until the liquid evaporates and the flavors are blended, about 2 minutes longer.

Per serving: 328 Cal, 10 g Fat, 2 g Sat Fat, 159 mg Chol, 642 mg Sod, 48 g Carb, 3 g Fib, 11 g Prot, 81 mg Calc. *POINTS: 7.*

cooking flash

To clean leeks, chop off the green tops, then slice horizontally through the white part almost to the root end. Rinse out the sand and grit under running water, then shake off the excess water.

Shrimp Couscous

MAKES 4 SERVINGS

Couscous, a pre-cooked grain that's ready in minutes, is available in specialty food stores and most large supermarkets. Substitute a pound of whole bay scallops or quartered sea scallops for the shrimp, if you like.

2 teaspoons olive oil
1 onion, chopped
1 medium zucchini, chopped
2 garlic cloves, minced
1 tablespoon thyme leaves
¼ teaspoon crushed red pepper
1½ cups chicken broth
1 tomato, peeled, seeded, and finely chopped
1 pound medium shrimp, peeled and deveined
1 cup couscous

Heat a nonstick skillet. Swirl in the oil, then add the onion and zucchini. Sauté until the onion is golden. Stir in the garlic and sauté until fragrant. Add the thyme, crushed red pepper, and broth; bring to a boil. Stir in the tomato and shrimp and return to a boil, then stir in the couscous. Remove from the heat, cover, and let stand until the shrimp turn pink and all the liquid is absorbed, about 5 minutes. Fluff with a fork before serving.

Per serving: 345 Cal, 6 g Fat, 1 g Sat Fat, 174 mg Chol, 552 mg Sod, 40 g Carb, 4 g Fib, 30 g Prot, 93 mg Calc. *POINTS: 7.*

Chicken Couscous

MAKES 4 SERVINGS

Dried fruit and warm spices such as ginger, cayenne, and cinnamon are common in Moroccan cooking.

1½ teaspoons ground cumin
½ teaspoon ground ginger
¼ teaspoon cinnamon
⅛ teaspoon cayenne pepper
1 pound skinless boneless chicken breasts, cut into strips
1 tablespoon olive oil
1 red bell pepper, seeded and chopped
4 scallions, sliced
½ cup golden raisins
½ cup orange juice
1 teaspoon salt
1¾ cups water
1 (5.7-ounce) box couscous

1. Mix the cumin, ginger, cinnamon, and cayenne in a large zip-close plastic bag. Add the chicken and shake to coat.

2. Heat the oil in a large nonstick skillet, then add the chicken. Sauté until cooked through, about 8 minutes. Transfer the chicken to a plate and keep warm.

3. In the skillet, sauté the bell pepper and scallions until softened. Stir in the raisins, orange juice, salt, and water; bring to a boil. Stir in the couscous. Remove from the heat, cover, and let stand until the liquid is absorbed, about 5 minutes. Add the chicken; mix thoroughly with a fork.

Per serving: 406 Cal, 7 g Fat, 1 g Sat Fat, 69 mg Chol, 604 mg Sod, 53 g Carb, 5 g Fib, 32 g Prot, 58 mg Calc.
POINTS: 8.

cooking flash

If you'd like a more robust dish, lamb is an excellent substitute for the chicken.

Minted Couscous Tabbouleh with Chickpeas and Feta

MAKES 4 SERVINGS

Tabbouleh is traditionally made with bulgur (cracked wheat), but couscous makes a speedy substitute. Serve this with pita wedges for a light supper, or buy prepared hummus and create a mezze platter.

 1 **cup couscous**
1½ **cups boiling water**
 1 **cup canned chickpeas, rinsed**
   and drained
12 **cherry tomatoes, halved**
¾ **cup minced flat-leaf parsley**
 4 **scallions, sliced**
⅓ **cup chopped mint**
½ **cup crumbled feta cheese**
 3 **tablespoons fresh lemon juice**
 4 **teaspoons extra-virgin olive oil**
½ **teaspoon Dijon mustard**
½ **teaspoon salt**

1. Put the couscous into a large heatproof bowl and add the boiling water. Cover tightly with foil and let stand until the water is absorbed, 5–10 minutes. Stir in the chickpeas, tomatoes, parsley, scallions, mint, and feta cheese.

2. Combine the lemon juice, oil, mustard, and salt in a glass jar. Cover the jar and shake to blend. Pour over the couscous and toss to combine.

Per serving: 376 Cal, 10 g Fat, 3 g Sat Fat, 14 mg Chol, 485 mg Sod, 57 g Carb, 5 g Fib, 15 g Prot, 154 mg Calc. *POINTS: 7.*

Italian-Flag Polenta

MAKES 4 SERVINGS

When this dish is served, the spinach, tomatoes, and mozzarella, atop the polenta base, represent the colors of the Italian flag.

2 (10-ounce) boxes frozen
   chopped spinach
2 (8-ounce) jars tomato sauce
1 (1-pound) log polenta, cut into
   12 slices
¾ cup shredded skim-milk
   mozzarella cheese
1 tablespoon olive oil

1. Cook the spinach according to package directions; drain thoroughly and set aside.
2. Preheat the oven to 375°F. Spray a 9 x 13–inch baking dish with nonstick spray. Spread 1 jar of the tomato sauce over the bottom of the dish. Set the polenta slices in a single layer over the tomato sauce, then top evenly with the spinach. Sprinkle with the shredded mozzarella, then top with the remaining jar of tomato sauce; drizzle with the oil. Bake until the cheese and sauce are bubbling, about 15 minutes. Let stand 5 minutes before serving.

Per serving: 308 Cal, 11 g Fat, 2 g Sat Fat, 2 mg Chol, 603 mg Sod, 40 g Carb, 7 g Fib, 15 g Prot, 319 mg Calc. **POINTS: 6.**

4 Foods No Cook Should Be Without

Need dinner, but no time to shop? Your cupboard will never truly be bare if you keep these on hand:

1. Frozen chopped spinach Easily thawed in the microwave, this handy veggie can be layered onto a prebaked pizza crust, tucked into a tortilla with salsa and cheese, blended into beaten eggs for a tasty omelet or quiche, or stuffed into refrigerated pizza dough and baked into quick calzones.

2. Plain fat-free yogurt Dollop some on a baked potato instead of sour cream. Use it as a substitute for mayonnaise in dips and salads, and stir it into cold or warm (not hot) soups to add creamy richness.

3. A wedge of Parmesan cheese When bought whole and grated as needed, this richly flavored cheese goes with just about anything and lasts many months in the fridge. Grate a little onto cooked vegetables or into salads, or sprinkle it on the top of a casserole.

4. A package of flour tortillas Keep on hand to turn leftovers and salads into tasty wraps, or to top with salsa and cheese for quick quesadillas. Top them with veggies and a little shredded cheese for pizza-in-a-pinch.

flash in the pan
stir-fries &
skillet suppers

Chicken Breasts Florentine

Chicken Breasts Florentine

MAKES 4 SERVINGS

The Italian city of Florence is associated with spinach, so dishes that feature the green are frequently named Florentine.

1 (10-ounce) bag triple-washed spinach, rinsed (do not dry)
1 garlic clove, minced
Freshly ground pepper, to taste
2 ounces lean ham, cut into strips
¼ teaspoon dried thyme
4 (¼-pound) skinless boneless chicken breast halves
4 teaspoons olive oil
½ cup dry white wine
¼ teaspoon salt

1. Heat a nonstick skillet and combine the spinach, garlic, and pepper. Cover and cook until the spinach wilts, about 2 minutes. Let cool and squeeze out excess liquid. Stir in the ham and a pinch of the thyme.
2. Cut a long thin pocket into each chicken breast. Stuff the spinach mixture into the pockets, then press the edges together and seal closed with toothpicks.
3. Heat the oil in the skillet, then add the chicken breasts and brown, turning once or twice. Add the wine, salt, and remaining thyme. Reduce the heat to low and simmer, covered, until the chicken is cooked through, about 10 minutes. Top with any pan juices and serve.

Per serving: 181 Cal, 6 g Fat, 1 g Sat Fat, 57 mg Chol, 447 mg Sod, 3 g Carb, 1 g Fib, 24 g Prot, 70 mg Calc.
POINTS: 4.

Seared Tuna with Onions and Anchovies

MAKES 4 SERVINGS

Don't be alarmed that this recipe calls for cooking the tuna until it's just rare. Tuna is similar to beef in that it can be enjoyed rare, medium, or well-done. If you prefer, cook the fish three to four minutes on each side for medium, four to five minutes on each side for well-done.

2 **onions, thinly sliced**
½ **cup dry white wine**
2 **garlic cloves, minced**
2 **teaspoons olive oil**
4 **(6-ounce) tuna steaks (1-inch thick)**
4 **plum tomatoes, peeled, seeded, and chopped**
¼ **cup chopped flat-leaf parsley**
1 **tablespoon white-wine vinegar**
4 **anchovy fillets, rinsed and chopped, or 2 teaspoons anchovy paste**
½ **teaspoon crushed red pepper**

1. Spray a nonstick skillet with nonstick spray and set over medium heat. Add the onions, wine, and garlic. Sauté until the onions are transparent.

2. Meanwhile, heat another nonstick skillet. Swirl in the oil, then add the tuna. Sear until done to taste, 2–3 minutes on each side for rare.

3. As soon as the tuna is turned, add the tomatoes, parsley, vinegar, anchovies, and crushed red pepper to the onions; heat to serving temperature, stirring constantly. Top the tuna with the vegetables and serve.

Per serving: 279 Cal, 10 g Fat, 2 g Sat Fat, 56 mg Chol, 209 mg Sod, 6 g Carb, 1 g Fib, 35 g Prot, 30 mg Calc.
POINTS: 6.

Smoked Whitefish Hash

MAKES 4 SERVINGS

Flavorful smoked fish replaces fatty corned beef in this healthy hash. Try smoked bass, scallops, trout, or tuna in place of the whitefish, or use smoked chicken or turkey. Serve hot sauce on the side, and lemon wedges instead of adding lemon juice to the hash, if desired.

½ tablespoon olive oil

2 large red potatoes, cut into ¼-inch cubes

1 white onion, cut into ¼-inch cubes

½ teaspoon salt

¼ teaspoon coarsely ground pepper

⅓ cup finely chopped green bell pepper

⅓ cup finely chopped yellow bell pepper

½ teaspoon chopped seeded jalapeño pepper (wear gloves to prevent irritation)

½ pound smoked whitefish, cut into chunks

½ cup fat-free half-and-half

¾ teaspoon dried thyme

2 teaspoons fresh lemon juice

Heat a nonstick skillet. Swirl in the oil, then add the potatoes, onion, salt, and ground pepper. Sauté until the potatoes begin to brown, then add the bell peppers and jalapeño. Sauté until the bell peppers are soft, 2–3 minutes. Add the whitefish, half-and-half, and thyme and cook until the half-and-half is absorbed, 3–4 minutes. Stir in the lemon juice and serve.

Per serving: 212 Cal, 2 g Fat, 0 g Sat Fat, 19 mg Chol, 907 mg Sod, 30 g Carb, 3 g Fib, 16 g Prot, 36 mg Calc. *POINTS: 4.*

Sautéed Prawns

MAKES 4 SERVINGS

If you like, add an ounce of chopped pancetta or two slices of diced bacon along with the prawns, as they do in Italy. If your supermarket doesn't carry prawns (which are a kind of freshwater shrimp), use jumbo shrimp instead.

1 pound large freshwater prawns
2 teaspoons olive oil
1 tablespoon chopped sage
2 bay leaves, crumbled
2 garlic cloves, minced
½ cup fresh lemon juice
½ teaspoon salt
Pinch crushed red pepper

1. With scissors, slit each prawn through the shell along the outer curve. Rinse under cold water to remove the veins. Combine the prawns, oil, sage, and bay leaves in a bowl.

2. Heat a nonstick skillet, then add the prawns and marinade. Cook until the prawns are opaque in the centers and the shells are bright pink all over, about 3 minutes on each side. Add the garlic, lemon juice, salt, and crushed red pepper and toss to combine.

Per serving: 168 Cal, 4 g Fat, 0 g Sat Fat, 0 mg Chol, 291 mg Sod, 10 g Carb, 0 g Fib, 22 g Prot, 69 mg Calc. *POINTS: 4.*

Shrimp in Marinara Sauce

MAKES 4 SERVINGS

Alone or with pasta, this dish is quick, easy, and delicious—the perfect recipe to turn to when you need last-minute company or family fare.

- **4 teaspoons olive oil**
- **1¼ pounds large shrimp, peeled and deveined**
- **2 garlic cloves, minced**
- **1 cup drained canned plum tomatoes (no salt added)**
- **1 cup dry white wine**
- **2 tablespoons minced flat-leaf parsley**
- **2 tablespoons tomato paste (no salt added)**
- **1 tablespoon minced fresh oregano, or ½ teaspoon dried**
- **¼ teaspoon salt**
- **¼ teaspoon crushed red pepper**

Heat the oil in a nonstick skillet, then add the shrimp and garlic. Sauté until the shrimp are pink. Stir in the tomatoes, wine, parsley, tomato paste, oregano, salt, and crushed red pepper. Bring to a boil and cook, stirring frequently, until the sauce is thickened, about 8 minutes. Serve at once.

Per serving: 224 Cal, 7 g Fat, 1 g Sat Fat, 174 mg Chol, 322 mg Sod, 6 g Carb, 1 g Fib, 24 g Prot, 93 mg Calc. *POINTS: 5.*

cooking flash

Although you can buy special gadgets designed to remove the veins from shrimp, they aren't necessary (in fact, the vein is edible, although unsightly and often gritty). One easy way to remove the vein is to stick a pair of scissors under the shell on the back of the shrimp, just deep enough to get the bit of flesh that covers the vein, and cut toward the tail. Peel off the shell, then rinse out the vein under cool water or remove it with your fingers.

Ginger Stir-Fried Monkfish

MAKES 4 SERVINGS

Oyster sauce, found in the Asian section of most supermarkets, imparts richness and creaminess to this stir-fry. Robust fresh ginger lends a pungent peppery accent (do not substitute ground ginger). Serve over white rice.

**1 pound monkfish, cut into
1½-inch cubes
1 tablespoon reduced-sodium soy sauce
1 teaspoon + 1 tablespoon cornstarch
⅔ cup vegetable broth
¼ cup + 2 tablespoons oyster sauce
2 tablespoons dry sherry
½ teaspoon sugar
1 (6-ounce) package sliced portobello
mushrooms, halved
½ pound asparagus spears, cut into
2-inch pieces on the diagonal
¼ pound snow peas
¼ cup water
½ tablespoon canola oil
½ tablespoon grated peeled fresh ginger
1 large garlic clove, minced**

1. Combine the monkfish, soy sauce, and 1 teaspoon of the cornstarch in a bowl. Set aside to marinate. For the sauce, mix together the broth, oyster sauce, sherry, sugar, and the remaining tablespoon of cornstarch in a second bowl.

2. Heat a nonstick wok or a large nonstick skillet over very high heat. Add the mushrooms and stir-fry until browned, about 4 minutes, then transfer to a plate. Add the asparagus, snow peas, and water. Stir-fry until bright green, about 3 minutes, then transfer to the plate.

3. Reheat the pan over high heat. Swirl in the oil. Stirring constantly, add the ginger and garlic, then the fish and marinade. Stir-fry until the fish is opaque, about 2 minutes. Return the vegetables to the pan, add the sauce, and stir-fry to heat through, about 2 minutes.

Per serving: 164 Cal, 4 g Fat, 1 g Sat Fat, 28 mg Chol, 511 mg Sod, 12 g Carb, 4 g Fib, 21 g Prot, 57 mg Calc.
POINTS: 3.

cooking flash

For this stir-fry be sure to get the pan good and hot and keep the food moving with a wooden spoon or paddle.

Ginger Stir-Fried Monkfish

Potato and Turkey Lyonnaise

MAKES 4 SERVINGS

In the center of France lies Lyons, a city known for its excellent food, particularly dishes featuring onions. Our Lyonnaise dish, turkey and potatoes, makes a tasty skillet meal.

- 2 **pounds red potatoes, scrubbed and sliced**
- ¾ **teaspoon salt**
- 4 **teaspoons olive oil**
- 10 **ounces skinless boneless turkey breast, cut into thin strips**
- 2 **onions, very thinly sliced**
- 2 **teaspoons chopped rosemary leaves**
- ½ **teaspoon freshly ground pepper**
- ¼ **teaspoon sugar**
- **Rosemary sprigs**

1. Cook the potatoes with ¼ teaspoon of the salt in water to cover until just tender, about 5 minutes. Pour off the water.

2. Heat 2 teaspoons of the oil in a nonstick skillet. Add the turkey and the remaining ½ teaspoon of salt and sauté until the turkey is no longer pink. Transfer to a plate.

3. Heat the remaining 2 teaspoons of oil in the skillet. Add the onions, rosemary, pepper, and sugar and sauté until the onions are softened. Add the potatoes and cook, stirring gently, until they are browned and very tender. Return the turkey to the skillet and heat through. Garnish with the rosemary sprigs and serve.

Per serving: 313 Cal, 5 g Fat, 1 g Sat Fat, 44 mg Chol, 463 mg Sod, 46 g Carb, 5 g Fib, 23 g Prot, 45 mg Calc. *POINTS: 6.*

cooking flash

If at all possible, avoid using dried rosemary in this dish. Its flavor is much more strident than fresh, and it has the texture of pine needles.

Seared Chicken Breasts and Potatoes

 MAKES 4 SERVINGS

Chicken and potatoes are a classic combination. In this quick preparation, we use chicken breast halves for speed and convenience.

½ **tablespoon olive oil**

4 **(¼-pound) skinless boneless chicken breast halves**

4 **small red potatoes, thinly sliced**

6 **kalamata olives, pitted and quartered**

1 **tablespoon chopped basil**

1. Heat a nonstick skillet. Swirl in the oil, then add the chicken breasts in a single layer. Sear until browned, about 2 minutes on each side. Transfer to a plate.

2. Add the potatoes to the skillet and cook, stirring occasionally, until they begin to brown. Stir in the olives and basil, then return the chicken to the pan. Reduce the heat to the lowest possible setting, cover, and cook until the chicken is cooked through and the potatoes are well browned, about 5 minutes longer, stirring the potatoes after 2–3 minutes.

Per serving: 256 Cal, 5 g Fat, 1 g Sat Fat, 66 mg Chol, 173 mg Sod, 24 g Carb, 2 g Fib, 28 g Prot, 25 mg Calc. *POINTS: 5.*

Quick Chicken Cacciatore

MAKES 4 SERVINGS

The classic version of this dish is made with bone-in chicken pieces. Using skinless boneless breasts lowers the fat and quickens the cooking time. Serve this dish with orzo or another small-shape pasta, or with couscous.

3 **tablespoons all-purpose flour**
½ **teaspoon salt**
¼ **teaspoon freshly ground pepper**
4 **(¼-pound) skinless boneless chicken breast halves**
1 **tablespoon olive oil**
2 **onions, chopped**
2 **garlic cloves, chopped**
1 **(8-ounce) package sliced mushrooms**
½ **cup dry red wine**
1 **(14½-ounce) can stewed tomatoes**

1. Mix the flour, ¼ teaspoon of the salt, and the pepper on a sheet of wax paper or a plate. Dredge the chicken in the flour mixture, shaking off the excess.

2. Heat the oil in a large nonstick skillet, then add the chicken. Cook until golden brown, about 4 minutes on each side. Transfer to a plate.

3. Add the onions and garlic to the skillet and sauté until softened. Add the mushrooms and sauté until they soften. Add the wine and cook, stirring, until the liquid evaporates. Stir in the tomatoes and the remaining ¼ teaspoon of salt, then return the chicken to the skillet. Reduce the heat, cover, and simmer until the chicken is cooked through, about 8 minutes.

Per serving: 271 Cal, 7 g Fat, 1 g Sat Fat, 69 mg Chol, 555 mg Sod, 19 g Carb, 3 g Fib, 28 g Prot, 67 mg Calc. **POINTS: 5.**

cooking flash

To cut down on prep time, use one cup of thawed frozen chopped onions instead of fresh.

Spanish Chicken with Rice and Beans

MAKES 4 SERVINGS

This satisfying one-dish meal is best served the day it is made.

1 **green bell pepper, seeded and chopped**
1 **onion, chopped**
2 **garlic cloves, minced**
¾ **pound skinless boneless chicken breasts, cubed**
1 **cup low-sodium chicken broth**
2 **tablespoons tomato paste**
1 **cup quick-cooking white rice**
1 **cup drained canned whole plum tomatoes**
⅔ **cup canned red kidney beans, rinsed and drained**
Freshly ground pepper, to taste

1. Spray a nonstick skillet with nonstick spray and set over medium-high heat. Sauté the bell pepper, onion, and garlic until softened. Add the chicken and sauté until browned.

2. Stir in the broth and tomato paste, then add the rice, tomatoes, beans, and ground pepper. Reduce the heat, cover, and simmer until most of the broth is absorbed, about 10 minutes. Uncover and cook, stirring occasionally, 5 minutes longer.

Per serving: 344 Cal, 3 g Fat, 0 g Sat Fat, 41 mg Chol, 271 mg Sod, 54 g Carb, 4 g Fib, 26 g Prot, 71 mg Calc. *POINTS: 6.*

Curried Chicken Nuggets with Spinach

  MAKES 4 SERVINGS

In India, spices like ginger are considered digestives. Try this dish with a bit more paprika, if you dare.

4 teaspoons olive oil

2 teaspoons ground cumin

1 teaspoon turmeric

½ teaspoon ground ginger

⅛ teaspoon hot Hungarian paprika

¾ pound skinless boneless chicken breasts, cut into 1-inch pieces

4 cups coarsely chopped cleaned spinach

2 tablespoons canned chopped green chiles

2 garlic cloves, minced

¾ cup canned chickpeas, rinsed and drained

2 tablespoons chili sauce

Heat the oil in a large nonstick skillet, then add the cumin, turmeric, ginger, and paprika. Sauté 1 minute, then add the chicken and sauté until cooked through, 6–8 minutes. Stir in the spinach, chiles, and garlic; cook until the spinach wilts, then stir in the chickpeas and chili sauce. Reduce the heat and simmer until the chickpeas are heated through, 2–3 minutes.

Per serving: 243 Cal, 7 g Fat, 1 g Sat Fat, 41 mg Chol, 211 mg Sod, 22 g Carb, 3 g Fib, 24 g Prot, 107 mg Calc. *POINTS: 5.*

cooking flash

Sautéing the spices heightens their flavor yet also mellows them so they don't taste as harsh.

Wiener Schnitzel

MAKES 2 SERVINGS

This traditional German dish is typically served with a delicate buttery-textured pasta called spaetzle, which means "little sparrow." Look for spaetzle in specialty stores and the ethnic-foods section of your supermarket.

½ **cup plain dried bread crumbs**
¼ **cup all-purpose flour**
2 **egg whites**
¼ **cup low-fat (1%) milk**
2 **(¼-pound) veal cutlets, pounded very thin**
2 **teaspoons vegetable oil**

1. Place the bread crumbs and flour in 2 separate shallow dishes. In a third shallow dish, beat the egg whites and milk. One at time, dip the cutlets into the flour, shaking off any excess; dip into the egg white mixture, then into the bread crumbs, pressing the crumbs to coat.
2. In a large nonstick skillet, heat 1 teaspoon of the oil. Cook one cutlet until golden brown, about 3 minutes, then turn and cook 1–2 minutes longer. Transfer to a plate and keep warm. Repeat with the remaining teaspoon of oil and cutlet.

Per serving: 377 Cal, 12 g Fat, 4 g Sat Fat, 91 mg Chol, 385 mg Sod, 32 g Carb, 2 g Fib, 32 g Prot, 121 mg Calc. **POINTS: 8.**

Breading Basics

Breading usually consists of dipping the food in a binder (a wet ingredient like milk or egg), coating it with a dry ingredient (like bread crumbs, cracker crumbs, or cornmeal), then cooking in a little oil.

• Before you begin, blot the food's surface to remove any moisture. Some cooks recommend dipping in flour before dipping in the binder.

• Don't skimp on the binder—it gives the coating something to cling to—but don't use too much or the coating may become soggy. Let any excess binder drain off before you dip the food in the coating.

• Use one hand to dip the food in the binder and the other to cover it with the coating.

• After covering the food with the coating, pat it with your fingers to help the coating stick.

• If you have the time, refrigerate the breaded food for ½ hour before cooking to help the coating adhere.

• When cooking breaded food, turn carefully. Gently work a pancake turner with a very thin blade under the food. Rest another turner on top of the food and flip, then gently slide out the bottom turner.

**Beef with Asparagus
and Cherry Tomatoes**

Beef with Asparagus and Cherry Tomatoes

MAKES 4 SERVINGS

This is a quick and very colorful meal. For a change of pace, substitute sugar-snap peas or green beans for the asparagus. Serve over noodles or rice pilaf.

24 **asparagus spears, cut diagonally into 1-inch pieces**
¼ **cup water**
10 **ounces lean boneless sirloin steak, cut into ¼-inch strips**
½ **teaspoon salt**
¼ **teaspoon freshly ground pepper**
4 **scallions, thinly sliced on the diagonal**
1 **large garlic clove, thinly sliced**
24 **cherry tomatoes, halved**

1. Combine the asparagus and water in a skillet and bring to a boil. Reduce the heat, cover, and simmer until the asparagus is tender, about 2 minutes. Pour off the water.
2. Sprinkle the beef with the salt and pepper; add it to the asparagus along with the scallions and garlic. Sauté until the beef is cooked through. Add the tomatoes and sauté until heated through, about 2 minutes longer.

Per serving: 129 Cal, 4 g Fat, 1 g Sat Fat, 43 mg Chol, 324 mg Sod, 7 g Carb, 2 g Fib, 18 g Prot, 39 mg Calc.
POINTS: 3.

cooking flash

For an Asian variation of this dish, add one teaspoon of grated ginger with the garlic and scallions. Drain a can of sliced water chestnuts and add it instead of the cherry tomatoes.

Speedy Chicken Stir-Fry

MAKES 4 SERVINGS

Watercress is most commonly used in salads; if you've never had it cooked, it tastes like slightly peppery spinach. This simple Chinese stir-fry is also delicious with tender baby spinach or bok choy leaves. To compliment the meal, serve quick-cooking barley on the side.

2 **teaspoons peanut oil**
1 **cup thinly sliced shiitake mushrooms**
1 **garlic clove, minced**
2 **bunches watercress, tough stems removed (about 8 cups)**
1 **(8-ounce) can sliced water chestnuts, drained**
1 **(8-ounce) can sliced bamboo shoots, drained**
2 **teaspoons sugar**
1 **teaspoon soy sauce**
1 **cup shredded cooked chicken breast**

1. In a large nonstick skillet or wok, heat the oil. Add the mushrooms and garlic; stir-fry until the mushrooms are wilted, 3–4 minutes. Add the watercress, water chestnuts, and bamboo shoots; stir-fry until the watercress is slightly wilted, about 30 seconds. Sprinkle with the sugar and soy sauce; cook, stirring gently, until the sugar dissolves, about 1 minute. With a slotted spoon, transfer the vegetables to a bowl; leave the liquid in the skillet.

2. Bring the liquid to a simmer; add the chicken. Pour in any liquid that has accumulated around the vegetables in the bowl. Stir-fry until the chicken is heated through, 2–3 minutes. Add to the vegetables; toss to combine.

Per serving: 107 Cal, 5 g Fat, 1 g Sat Fat, 29 mg Chol, 140 mg Sod, 5 g Carb, 2 g Fib, 12 g Prot, 89 mg Calc.
POINTS: 2.

cooking flash

Barley has a hearty flavor and pleasantly chewy texture, but it is rather slow-cooking. It usually needs to simmer for close to an hour. Quick-cooking barley can be on the table in 10 minutes—less time than it takes to make traditional white rice. Look for it near the hot cereals in your supermarket.

Stir-Fried Pork with Vegetables

MAKES 4 SERVINGS

Try this colorful and easy entrée using any of your favorite vegetables. Serve over an aromatic rice like basmati or jasmine.

2 teaspoons olive oil
1 large onion, chopped
2 cups broccoli florets
¼ cup water
1 red bell pepper, seeded and cut into 1-inch pieces
1 small zucchini, halved lengthwise and cut into 1-inch pieces
1 cup sugar-snap peas
10 ounces lean boneless pork loin, cut into ¼-inch strips
1 teaspoon thyme leaves
¼ teaspoon salt
Pinch freshly ground pepper
1 tablespoon white-wine vinegar

1. Heat the oil in a nonstick skillet. Add the onion and sauté until softened. Add the broccoli and water, then cover and cook until the broccoli is tender, about 5 minutes. Stir in the bell pepper, zucchini, and peas, then cover and cook until the bell pepper is tender, about 2 minutes longer.

2. Add the pork, thyme, salt, and ground pepper to the vegetables. Sauté until the pork is browned, then stir in the vinegar. Cook, stirring, until the pork is cooked through, about 2 minutes longer.

Per serving: 190 Cal, 7 g Fat, 2 g Sat Fat, 42 mg Chol, 226 mg Sod, 14 g Carb, 5 g Fib, 20 g Prot, 82 mg Calc. *POINTS: 4.*

Spicy Tofu with Broccoli and Cashews

MAKES 4 SERVINGS

This delicious veggie-lovers stir-fry is packed with nutrition. Serve it with aromatic rice and some mandarin orange slices to enhance the Asian flavors and ambiance.

- 2 teaspoons vegetable oil
- 1 head broccoli, trimmed and cut into bite-size pieces
- 5–6 scallions, cut into 2-inch lengths (keep white and green parts separate)
- ½ cup fat-free vegetable or chicken broth
- 1 tablespoon reduced-sodium soy sauce
- 2 teaspoons cornstarch
- 1 teaspoon sugar
- ¼ teaspoon crushed red pepper flakes
- 1 (10½-ounce) package low-fat firm tofu, cut into 1-inch cubes
- ½ cup dry-roasted cashews

1. In a very large nonstick skillet or wok with a lid, heat the oil over high heat. Add the broccoli and the white scallions bulbs; stir-fry 1 minute. Add all but 1 tablespoon of the broth; bring to a boil. Reduce the heat and simmer, covered, 2 minutes.

2. In a small bowl, mix the remaining tablespoon of broth, the soy sauce, cornstarch, sugar, and pepper flakes. Pour over the vegetables and stir until they are coated. Simmer, uncovered, until the liquid thickens, about 1 minute. Add the tofu, cashews, and green scallion tops. Simmer, covered, until the tofu is heated through, about 1 minute.

Per serving: 184 Cal, 12 g Fat, 2 g Sat Fat, 0 mg Chol, 186 mg Sod, 11 g Carb, 1 g Fib, 9 g Prot, 43 mg Calc. **POINTS: 4.**

cooking flash

If you have time to plan ahead, press the tofu to give it a firmer texture: Cut the tofu in half lengthwise and place it between 2 plates. Place a heavy can on the top plate (the sides of the tofu should bulge slightly) and let stand for no more than 1 hour. Drain off the liquid and refrigerate the tofu for up to 2 days; cut it into cubes just before using.

Spicy Tofu with
Broccoli and Cashews

Molasses-Glazed Ham Steak

MAKES 4 SERVINGS

A simple, sweet glaze really wakes up the taste of ham. Add sliced tomatoes and corn on the cob for a fast and easy summer supper.

3 tablespoons molasses
2 tablespoons packed brown sugar
1 tablespoon Dijon mustard
2 teaspoons cider vinegar
1 (1-pound) ham steak, trimmed of all fat

1. Spray a nonstick ridged grill pan with nonstick cooking spray and set over medium–high heat.
2. Combine the molasses, brown sugar, mustard, and vinegar. Put the ham in the grill pan and cook, brushing frequently with the glaze, until lightly browned, about 4 minutes on each side.

Per serving: 232 Cal, 6 g Fat, 2 g Sat Fat, 60 mg Chol, 1,342 mg Sod, 18 g Carb, 0 g Fib, 24 g Prot, 44 mg Calc. *POINTS: 5.*

Sautéing and Searing the Right Way

• When you sauté, you're cooking foods over medium-high to high heat in a small amount of oil; you're also stirring very frequently to keep the food from scorching. Searing differs in one regard: You don't stir, so the food (typically a cut of meat or fish) develops a crust.

• When searing, be sure the food is as dry as possible (blot meats dry with a paper towel). Water or moisture will spatter on contact with the hot oil, and it can cause the food to steam, inhibiting the formation of a crust.

• Dark pans will cause faster browning because they absorb heat. Choose them to caramelize onions or to get a nice crust on chops, steaks, or fillets.

• Light or shiny pans reflect heat, so foods brown much more slowly. Choose them for sautéing vegetables, making frittatas, or stir-frying.

• Heating the oil in the pan and then adding the food lowers the temperature of the pan and the oil significantly. Use this technique when the texture of the food is important (such as when you're sautéing onions until they soften) or the color is secondary (you're cooking cubed meat or poultry until no longer pink).

Pork Chops with Cider Vinegar Glaze

MAKES 4 SERVINGS

Cider vinegar and sage team up to make a luscious glaze for these pork chops. Serve this with parsleyed orzo or egg noodles along with roasted Brussels sprouts.

4 (3-ounce) boneless pork loin chops
¼ teaspoon freshly ground pepper
½ cup low-sodium chicken broth
¼ cup cider vinegar
Pinch ground sage
1 tablespoon chopped flat-leaf parsley

1. Sprinkle the chops on both sides with the pepper. Spray a skillet with nonstick spray and set over medium heat. Add the pork and cook over high heat until browned, about 3 minutes on each side.

2. Add the broth, vinegar, and sage to the chops; bring to a boil. Reduce the heat and simmer, turning the chops once, until the pork is cooked through and the sauce is slightly thickened, about 5 minutes. Sprinkle with the parsley and serve.

Per serving: 129 Cal, 5 g Fat, 2 g Sat Fat, 50 mg Chol, 59 mg Sod, 1 g Carb, 0 g Fib, 19 g Prot, 19 mg Calc. *POINTS: 3.*

cooking flash

If you have one, use a dark skillet made of cast-iron or anodized aluminum. It retains heat well and cooks food evenly.

elegantly easy

Anchovy-Garlic Lamb Chops

Anchovy-Garlic Lamb Chops

MAKES 4 SERVINGS

Lamb and anchovies make a delightful marriage of flavors, as this quick dinner shows. Serve it with a medley of roasted vegetables.

4 (¼-pound) bone-in lamb chops, trimmed
Freshly ground pepper, to taste
2 anchovy fillets, rinsed and chopped
½ teaspoon grated lemon zest
1 teaspoon fresh lemon juice
2 garlic cloves, minced
¼ teaspoon Dijon mustard
⅛ teaspoon dried thyme leaves, crumbled
2 teaspoons olive oil
2 teaspoons minced parsley
Lemon thyme sprigs (optional)

1. Spray the broiler rack with nonstick spray. Preheat the broiler. Sprinkle the chops evenly with pepper and broil 5 inches from the heat until done to taste, 4–5 minutes on each side for medium.
2. Meanwhile, mash the anchovies, lemon zest, lemon juice, garlic, mustard, and dried thyme; gradually work in the oil. When the chops are done, brush the sauce over them. Sprinkle with the parsley, garnish with the lemon thyme (if you like), and serve.

Per serving: 148 Cal, 8 g Fat, 2 g Sat Fat, 55 mg Chol, 129 mg Sod, 0 g Carb, 0 g Fib, 18 g Prot, 18 mg Calc.
POINTS: 4.

cooking flash

Mash the anchovies with a mortar and pestle or in a small bowl with the back of a spoon.

Lamb Kebabs with Raisin Couscous

MAKES 4 SERVINGS

Moroccan cuisine is identifiable by the wide variety of spices—cumin, cinnamon, ginger, coriander, and turmeric—often combined into a mixture called ras al hanout, which is similar to the curry powder of Indian cuisine. It also often features fruit. This sweet and savory combination of lamb, yogurt, cumin, couscous, and raisins is typical of Moroccan-style dishes.

¾ **cup plain low-fat yogurt**
¾ **teaspoon salt**
½ **teaspoon ground cumin**
¼ **teaspoon paprika**
¾ **pound boneless lean lamb, trimmed of all visible fat and cut into 1-inch cubes**
1 **red bell pepper, seeded and cut into 1-inch pieces**
1 **medium zucchini or yellow squash, cut into ½-inch slices**
1¾ **cups chicken broth**
¼ **cup orange juice or water**
1 **(10-ounce) box plain couscous**
½ **cup golden or dark raisins**

1. Preheat the broiler. In a large bowl, mix the yogurt, ¼ teaspoon of the salt, the cumin and paprika. Stir in the lamb, bell pepper, and zucchini.
2. In a medium saucepan, bring the broth, orange juice, and the remaining ½ teaspoon of salt to a boil. Stir in the couscous and raisins. Remove from the heat; set aside, covered, until the liquid is absorbed, at least 5 minutes.
3. Thread the lamb, bell pepper, and zucchini alternately onto 4 metal skewers; discard the marinade. Broil the kebabs 3 inches from the heat, turning at least once, until the lamb is just cooked through, 10–12 minutes. Spoon the couscous onto a platter and top with the kebabs.

Per serving: 336 Cal, 9 g Fat, 4 g Sat Fat, 69 mg Chol, 970 mg Sod, 36 g Carb, 3 g Fib, 27 g Prot, 126 mg Calc. *POINTS: 7.*

cooking flash

Cut up the meat and vegetables while the broiler preheats, then thread them onto the skewers while the couscous cooks. Don't use bamboo skewers unless you have the time—at least 30 minutes—to soak them in water before using (otherwise they may catch fire).

Mandarin Beef Medallions

MAKES 4 SERVINGS

Soy sauce, rice vinegar, and ginger combine to give an Asian flavor to these quickly marinated steaks.

4 (¼-pound) beef tenderloin
  steaks, trimmed
3 tablespoons reduced-sodium
  soy sauce
3 tablespoons rice vinegar
3 tablespoons honey
4 teaspoons Asian (dark) sesame oil
1 garlic clove, minced
¼ teaspoon ground ginger
¼ teaspoon crushed red pepper
½ teaspoon salt

1. With your hands, gently press the steaks into ovals about ¾-inch thick.

2. Combine the soy sauce, vinegar, honey, oil, garlic, ginger, and crushed red pepper in a shallow baking dish. Add the steaks and turn to coat. Cover and let stand at room temperature 10 minutes.

3. Set a nonstick ridged grill pan over high heat. When a drop of water skitters when placed in the pan, transfer the steaks to the pan and sear 1 minute on each side. Reduce the heat to medium-high and sprinkle the steaks with the salt. Cook about 2–3 minutes on each side for rare, or until done to taste. Pour the marinade over the steaks and cook, turning steaks once or twice, until the sauce thickens to a light glaze. Remove from heat. Top the steaks with the glaze before serving.

Per serving: 278 Cal, 13 g Fat, 4 g Sat Fat, 71 mg Chol, 778 mg Sod, 15 g Carb, 0 g Fib, 25 g Prot, 13 mg Calc. *POINTS: 7.*

Sirloin with Tomatoes and Olives

MAKES 4 SERVINGS

Topping broiled steak with two quintessentially Mediterranean foods gives it a whole new flavor. Try the sauce over chicken or pasta, too. We like to serve the steak with mashed potatoes and caperberries (large stemmed capers imported from Spain).

1 (1-pound) lean boneless sirloin steak
4 plum tomatoes, chopped
12 kalamata olives, pitted and sliced
1 tablespoon minced fresh oregano, or ½ teaspoon dried
2 garlic cloves, minced
Freshly ground pepper, to taste

1. Preheat the broiler. Broil the steak 5 inches from the heat until done to taste, about 5 minutes on each side for rare. Transfer to a cutting board and let stand 5 minutes before slicing against the grain.
2. Meanwhile, spray a nonstick skillet with nonstick spray and set over medium heat. Add the tomatoes, olives, oregano, garlic, and pepper; cook, stirring frequently, until thickened, about 5 minutes. Serve the steak topped with the sauce.

Per serving: 198 Cal, 8 g Fat, 3 g Sat Fat, 76 mg Chol, 185 mg Sod, 4 g Carb, 1 g Fib, 26 g Prot, 30 mg Calc. *POINTS: 4.*

cooking flash

When meat is cooked, its juices come to the surface. Letting the steak stand before cutting it allows the juices to redistribute evenly throughout the meat, resulting in better flavor and texture.

Sirloin with Tomatoes and Olives

Creamy Beef and Noodles

MAKES 4 SERVINGS

This is a lighter version of the classic Beef Stroganoff. Crusty bread and a tossed salad are all you need to complete the meal.

  6 **ounces wide egg noodles**
10 **ounces lean boneless beef loin, cut into strips**
  1 **onion, thinly sliced**
  2 **cups small white mushrooms**
  1 **tablespoon unsalted butter**
  4 **teaspoons all-purpose flour**
  1 **cup low-sodium beef broth**
  1 **teaspoon Dijon mustard**
½ **teaspoon paprika**
½ **teaspoon salt**
¼ **teaspoon freshly ground pepper**
¼ **cup light sour cream**

1. Cook the noodles according to package directions. Drain and keep warm.
2. Meanwhile, brown the beef in a nonstick skillet. Transfer the beef to a plate. Spray the skillet with nonstick spray. Sauté the onion and mushrooms until browned. Transfer to the plate with the beef.
3. Melt the butter in the skillet, then sprinkle in the flour. Cook, stirring constantly, until bubbling. Continuing to stir, slowly pour in the broth, then add the mustard, paprika, salt, and pepper. Cook, stirring constantly, until thickened. Stir in the sour cream. Stir in the beef and vegetables and heat to serving temperature. Serve over the noodles.

Per serving: 282 Cal, 11 g Fat, 5 g Sat Fat, 91 mg Chol, 417 mg Sod, 19 g Carb, 2 g Fib, 26 g Prot, 48 mg Calc.
POINTS: 6.

Sage-Dusted Veal

MAKES 4 SERVINGS

Veal, sage, and white wine are a classic combination in Tuscany. Veal is so low in fat that it can dry out rapidly; watch it carefully so that it doesn't overcook. Because these cutlets are so flat, they need to be cooked in the largest skillet you have (or else in batches in a smaller one). For this meal, you might start with a savory mushroom soup and then serve roasted asparagus alongside the veal.

2 teaspoons olive oil

1 tablespoon all-purpose flour

1 teaspoon ground sage

¼ teaspoon salt

⅛ teaspoon freshly ground pepper

4 (4-ounce) thin-sliced veal cutlets (⅛-inch thick)

¼ cup dry white wine or chicken broth

1. In a very large (12-inch) nonstick skillet, heat the oil. In a large sealable plastic bag, mix the flour, sage, salt, and pepper. Add the veal and shake gently to coat.
2. Transfer the veal to the skillet, shaking off any excess flour (discard the remaining flour); sauté until cooked through, 2–3 minutes on each side. Add the wine; cook 1 minute longer. Serve at once.

Per serving: 162 Cal, 6 g Fat, 2 g Sat Fat, 91 mg Chol, 311 mg Sod, 2 g Carb, 0 g Fib, 23 g Prot, 23 mg Calc.
POINTS: 4.

cooking flash

For an easy and delicious mushroom soup, sauté any variety of sliced mushrooms until they are a deep, rich brown. Pour in beef broth and heat to serving temperature. For more heft, stir in some cooked rice or barley, or some cooked carrot slices.

Bocconcini di Vitello

MAKES 4 SERVINGS

Bocconcini most often refers to little balls of mozzarella cheese. But the word, Italian for "small mouthfuls," can also refer to other food, like the veal in this Italian classic. Serve with pasta or roasted potatoes.

4 teaspoons olive oil
1 pound boneless lean veal leg, cubed
1 (9-ounce) box frozen artichoke hearts, thawed
1 tomato, seeded and chopped
1 garlic clove, minced
2 teaspoons minced oregano
½ cup dry white wine
1 tablespoon minced parsley
¼ teaspoon salt
Freshly ground pepper, to taste

Heat a nonstick skillet. Swirl in 2 teaspoons of the oil, then add half of the veal. Sauté until well browned. Transfer to a plate. Repeat with the remaining oil and veal. Return the reserved veal to the skillet. Stir in the artichoke hearts, tomato, garlic, and oregano. Reduce the heat and simmer 2–3 minutes, then stir in the wine, parsley, salt, and pepper. Cook, partially covered, until the veal is tender, about 15 minutes. Top with the pan juices and serve.

Per serving: 217 Cal, 7 g Fat, 1 g Sat Fat, 83 mg Chol, 249 mg Sod, 9 g Carb, 4 g Fib, 25 g Prot, 33 mg Calc.
POINTS: 4.

Worth the Price

Here are five or our favorite convenience foods that make eating healthfully easy:

• **Prewashed bagged spinach** If you've ever washed a muddy bunch of spinach, you'll appreciate it when someone else has done the work for you. In minutes you can have a spinach salad, steamed spinach, or a spinach-based stir-fry.

• **Precut and baby carrots** Keep these in the fridge to grab when the crunchy-snack urge strikes; they're as easy to reach for as potato chips. They can also be microwaved for a colorful side dish.

• **Low-fat couscous or bean soup cups** Lunch- or dinner-for-one is as simple as microwaving a few minutes. Just be sure to check labels and buy only the low-fat, reduced-sodium types.

• **Frozen fish** If properly frozen and stored, frozen fish fillets often taste fresher than the "daily catch" at your supermarket. They make a great low-fat main dish, as long as you keep the toppings lean.

• **Calcium-fortified orange juice** This nutritional gem comes in convenient cartons—and tastes good, too. A nice break from dairy products, the juice's vitamin C helps you absorb the calcium better, to boot.

Wine-Poached Chicken with Tarragon Cream

MAKES 4 SERVINGS

Poaching chicken in wine and broth adds flavor and keeps the chicken moist. Try roasted broccoli and rice pilaf to round out the meal.

½ **cup fat-free sour cream**
4 **teaspoons reduced-calorie mayonnaise**
1 **tablespoon minced tarragon**
½ **teaspoon freshly ground pepper**
1 **cup low-sodium chicken broth**
¼ **cup dry white wine**
8 **peppercorns**
4 **tarragon sprigs**
1 **pound skinless boneless chicken breasts**

1. Mix the sour cream, mayonnaise, minced tarragon, and pepper in a small bowl. Cover and refrigerate.
2. Bring the broth, wine, peppercorns, and tarragon sprigs to a boil in a skillet. Add the chicken and bring back to a boil. Reduce the heat, cover, and poach the chicken at a gentle boil until cooked through, about 10 minutes. Transfer the chicken to a cutting board and let stand 5 minutes. Thinly slice the chicken. Serve with the tarragon cream on the side.

Per serving: 180 Cal, 5 g Fat, 1 g Sat Fat, 74 mg Chol, 118 mg Sod, 3 g Carb, 0 g Fib, 29 g Prot, 59 mg Calc.
POINTS: 4.

Brandied Chicken with Summer Fruits

Brandied Chicken with Summer Fruits

MAKES 4 SERVINGS

Nectarines and plums are at their peak in the summertime. This dish is prettiest with red plums, which develop a lovely jewel-like color when cooked. As a foil to the sweet fruit, serve with Brussels sprouts, quartered and quickly steamed.

¼ **cup + 2 tablespoons**
   all-purpose flour
½ **teaspoon salt**
½ **teaspoon freshly ground pepper**
¼ **teaspoon ground nutmeg**
4 **(¼-pound) skinless boneless**
   chicken breast halves
4 **teaspoons olive oil**
4 **scallions, very thinly sliced**
2 **garlic cloves, minced**
½ **cup brandy**
⅓ **cup low-sodium chicken broth**
½ **teaspoon sugar**
4 **plums, peeled and sliced**
2 **nectarines, peeled and sliced**

1. Combine the flour, salt, pepper, and nutmeg on a sheet of wax paper. Dredge the chicken in the mixture to coat all over.
2. Heat 2 teaspoons of the oil in a nonstick skillet, then add the scallions and garlic. Sauté until soft. Transfer to a plate.
3. Heat the remaining 2 teaspoons of oil in the skillet. Add the chicken and brown 3–4 minutes on each side. Stir in the brandy, broth, and sugar, then return the scallions to the pan. Bring to a boil, then add the plums. Reduce the heat, cover, and simmer until the chicken is cooked through, about 5 minutes. Add the nectarines and cook, stirring occasionally, until heated through.

Per serving: 362 Cal, 7 g Fat, 1 g Sat Fat, 66 mg Chol, 361 mg Sod, 35 g Carb, 3 g Fib, 29 g Prot, 45 mg Calc. *POINTS: 7.*

Chicken and Artichokes

MAKES 4 SERVINGS

This is a lightened-up variation of the French dish Chicken Archduke; we've omitted the cream and replaced the white wine with sherry. For a nice garnish, top with snipped chives.

2 teaspoons olive oil
4 (¼-pound) skinless boneless chicken breast halves
1 cup sliced shiitake mushrooms
1 small white onion, chopped
2 garlic cloves, minced
⅓ cup dry sherry
1 cup low-sodium chicken broth
1 (9-ounce) package frozen artichoke hearts, thawed

1. Heat 1 teaspoon of the oil in a nonstick skillet, then add the chicken. Sauté until browned, about 4 minutes on each side. Transfer to a plate. Add the mushrooms and sauté until softened, about 2 minutes. Transfer to the plate with the chicken. To the skillet, add the remaining teaspoon of oil and sauté the onion and garlic until the onion begins to brown. Add the sherry and cook until it is reduced by half, about 4 minutes. Add the broth and cook until the mixture is thick enough to coat the back of a spoon, 1–2 minutes.
2. Return the chicken and mushrooms to the pan and add the artichokes. Simmer until the chicken is cooked through, about 5 minutes; turn the chicken at least once to coat it with the sauce.

Per serving: 209 Cal, 4 g Fat, 1 g Sat Fat, 67 mg Chol, 134 mg Sod, 10 g Carb, 5 g Fib, 30 g Prot, 40 mg Calc.
POINTS: 4.

cooking flash
To serve this dish family style, use one pound of chicken tenders instead of whole chicken breasts.

Turkey Molé

MAKES 4 SERVINGS

Molé (pronounced mo-lay) is a spicy, dark brown Mexican sauce traditionally served with poultry. What goes in a molé is up to the cook, but it usually contains aromatic vegetables, seeds, spices and chiles, and a little unsweetened chocolate or cocoa powder for richness and color.

1 teaspoon vegetable oil
1 large onion, diced
2 garlic cloves, minced
½ cup golden raisins or chopped prunes
1 tablespoon unsweetened
  cocoa powder
1 tablespoon creamy peanut butter
2 teaspoons chili powder
¾ teaspoon salt
½ teaspoon cinnamon
⅛ teaspoon ground cloves
⅛ teaspoon anise or fennel seeds
4 (4-ounce) thin-sliced skinless
  turkey breasts (¼-inch thick)
2 tablespoons chopped cilantro
1 lime, quartered

1. In a small saucepan, heat the oil. Sauté the onion and garlic until tender, about 3 minutes. Stir in the raisins, cocoa powder, peanut butter, chili powder, ¼ teaspoon of the salt, the cinnamon, cloves, anise seeds, and 1 cup water. Simmer, covered, until the flavors are blended, about 20 minutes. Transfer to a blender and puree.

2. Meanwhile, spray a large nonstick skillet with nonstick cooking spray; heat. Sprinkle the turkey with the remaining ½ teaspoon of salt; sauté until cooked through, about 3 minutes on each side.

3. Spoon some of the sauce onto each of 4 plates. Top with the turkey and the remaining sauce. Sprinkle with the cilantro and serve with the lime on the side.

Per serving: 229 Cal, 4 g Fat, 1 g Sat Fat, 70 mg Chol, 508 mg Sod, 21 g Carb, 2 g Fib, 30 g Prot, 32 mg Calc.
POINTS: 5.

Grilled Quail with Lemon-Caper Sauce

MAKES 6 SERVINGS

Quail are sold frozen in some supermarkets and in Asian groceries; some butcher shops may carry them fresh. If you cook the quail in a ridged grill pan, cover the pan for the last 5 minutes of cooking after you turn the quail. Grilled polenta triangles and a wilted Swiss chard salad go nicely with the quail.

6 (¼-pound) quail, butterflied
3 tablespoons fresh lemon juice
½ tablespoon arrowroot
¼ teaspoon salt
⅛ teaspoon freshly ground pepper
1 cup dry white wine
2 large garlic cloves, minced
1 tablespoon large capers, drained

1. Preheat the broiler or grill, or set a nonstick ridged grill pan over high heat.
2. Spray the quail with nonstick spray and position them with the skin side facing the heat source. Brown 3 minutes, turn the birds over, and grill or broil until cooked through, about 5 minutes on the second side.
3. Meanwhile, mix the lemon juice, arrowroot, salt, and pepper in a small bowl. Combine the wine, garlic, and capers in a saucepan. Bring to a boil and keep boiling for 3 minutes. Remove from the heat and stir in the arrowroot mixture. Return to the stove and cook over low heat, stirring constantly, until the sauce is thickened and clear, about 2 minutes. Serve the quail, drizzled with the sauce. Remove the skin before eating.

Per serving: 83 Cal, 2 g Fat, 1 g Sat Fat, 26 mg Chol, 171 mg Sod, 2 g Carb, 0 g Fib, 8 g Prot, 12 mg Calc.
POINTS: 2.

cooking flash

To butterfly a quail, slit it open along the back bone with sturdy shears, place the skin side up on a cutting board, and gently press down on the breast bone to flatten.

Duck Fricassee

MAKES 4 SERVINGS

Be sure to use Muscovy duck breast, which has only a fraction of the fat of other varieties. Cipollini onions are the small, rather squat ones. If you can't find them, substitute pearl onions or large shallots.

1 **(14-ounce) Muscovy duck breast, skin scored in a crosshatch pattern**
4 **cipollini onions, quartered**
½ **fennel bulb, trimmed and sliced**
12 **baby carrots**
1 **tomato, peeled, seeded, and finely chopped**
4 **green olives, pitted and halved**
½ **cup dry white wine**

1. Heat a nonstick skillet. Brown the duck breast, skin-side down, about 3 minutes. Transfer to a plate and pour off any fat from the pan. Add the onions, fennel, and carrots and sauté until they just begin to brown, then reduce the heat and cook until fork-tender. Add the tomato and olives and cook, stirring, 1 minute longer. Pour in the wine, return the duck breast to the pan and cook, covered, until the duck is cooked through, about 8 minutes.
2. Transfer the duck to a cutting board, remove the skin, and slice on the diagonal. Divide the vegetables among 4 dinner plates and fan the duck slices on the side.

Per serving: 200 Cal, 5 g Fat, 1 g Sat Fat, 76 mg Chol, 182 mg Sod, 12 g Carb, 3 g Fib, 22 g Prot, 44 mg Calc. ***POINTS: 4.***

cooking flash

Crosshatching the skin of the duck serves two purposes: It helps to render the fat as well as brown and crisp the skin. Use only the white portion of the fennel bulb, but save some of the feathery green fronds for a colorful garnish.

Tuna Steaks Flambé with Sauce Diane

 MAKES 4 SERVINGS

Flambéing nicely chars the outside of the tuna steaks and burns off the alcohol from the cognac, leaving only a woody accent. This preparation is best rare, so choose high-quality ahi tuna, if available. Serve with pattypan squash and vegetable couscous.

4 (6-ounce) ahi tuna steaks
2 tablespoons cognac
Salt, to taste
Freshly ground pepper, to taste
½ tablespoon olive oil
1 garlic clove, minced
2 tablespoons dry red wine
½ cup chicken broth
½ teaspoon Worcestershire sauce
½ teaspoon Dijon mustard
1 teaspoon cornstarch
¼ cup fat-free half-and-half
½ teaspoon fresh lemon juice,
   or more to taste
Lemon zest and thyme sprigs (optional)

1. Preheat the oven to the lowest setting. Spray the steaks with olive oil cooking spray.
2. Heat a large nonstick skillet over medium-high heat. Add the tuna and sear until well browned, about 2 minutes on each side. Pour the cognac over the steaks. When it begins to bubble, carefully light the pan juices with a long kitchen match, gently shaking the pan until the flame has subsided. Transfer the tuna to an ovenproof platter, season with salt and pepper, and place in the oven to keep warm.
3. Swirl the oil into the skillet, then add the garlic. Sauté until fragrant, then add the wine and cook 1 minute, scraping up the browned bits from the bottom of the pan. Stir in the broth, Worcestershire sauce, and mustard. Bring to a boil while stirring; keep boiling until reduced by about half, about 3 minutes. Dissolve the cornstarch in the half-and-half. Stir the mixture into the pan and cook, stirring constantly, until heated through and thickened, about 1 minute. Stir in the lemon juice and spoon the sauce over the tuna steaks. Garnish with lemon zest and thyme sprigs, if you like.

Per serving: 240 Cal, 4 g Fat, 1 g Sat Fat, 77 mg Chol, 226 mg Sod, 3 g Carb, 0 g Fib, 40 g Prot, 32 mg Calc.
POINTS: 5.

Tuna Steaks Flambé with Sauce Diane

Mediterranean Shrimp

 MAKES 4 SERVINGS

Serve this over orzo with lemon wedges on the side. If you have any leftovers, stuff them into a pita for lunch the next day.

4 teaspoons olive oil
2 cups finely chopped peeled eggplant
1 red onion, chopped
3 garlic cloves, minced
6 plum tomatoes, finely chopped
½ cup dry white wine
1 tablespoon chopped oregano
   or marjoram
½ cup water
¾ pound medium shrimp, peeled
   and deveined
⅓ cup crumbled feta cheese
2 tablespoons chopped flat-leaf parsley

1. Heat the oil in a nonstick skillet. Add the eggplant and sauté until lightly browned. Stir in the onion and garlic and sauté until fragrant. Add the tomatoes, wine, oregano, and water, then bring to a boil. Reduce the heat and simmer, stirring occasionally, until most of the liquid evaporates.

2. Add the shrimp to the vegetables and cook, stirring frequently, until they turn pink. Sprinkle shrimp and vegetables with the feta and parsley and serve.

Per serving: 198 Cal, 8 g Fat, 2 g Sat Fat, 117 mg Chol, 235 mg Sod, 9 g Carb, 2 g Fib, 17 g Prot, 124 mg Calc.
POINTS: 4.

Garlicky Lemon Scallops

MAKES 4 SERVINGS

Be sure to pat the scallops dry before you mix them with the flour and salt. That way they won't soak up too much flour.

1 tablespoon olive oil

1¼ pounds sea scallops, dried with paper towels

2 tablespoons all-purpose flour

¼ teaspoon salt

4–6 garlic cloves, minced

1 scallion or large shallot, finely chopped

Pinch ground sage

Juice of 1 lemon (2–3 tablespoons)

2 tablespoons chopped parsley

1. In a large nonstick skillet, heat the oil. In a medium bowl, toss the scallops with the flour and salt.

2. Transfer the scallops to the skillet; add the garlic, scallion, and sage. Sauté until the scallops are just opaque, 3–4 minutes. Stir in the lemon juice and parsley; remove from the heat and serve at once.

Per serving: 187 Cal, 5 g Fat, 1 g Sat Fat, 47 mg Chol, 376 mg Sod, 10 g Carb, 1 g Fib, 25 g Prot, 51 mg Calc. *POINTS: 4.*

shopping flash

You can substitute the tiny bay or even tinier calico scallops for the larger sea scallops that we call for in the recipe. Bay scallops are sweeter, but many people prefer sea scallops because their flavor is more intense (they're also less expensive). If you do use the smaller scallops, be sure to reduce the cooking time to about a minute or two. Whichever type you use, watch them carefully lest they overcook and become tough and rubbery.

Trout Amandine

Trout Amandine

MAKES 4 SERVINGS

You don't need a lot of almonds to create the rich flavor essential to this famous dish—especially when they're toasted to enhance their flavor. Quartered green tomatoes and a quick slaw of radicchio, cabbage, and carrots are nice accompaniments.

3 **lemons**
½ **cup dry white wine**
¼ **cup minced parsley**
1 **teaspoon salt**
½ **teaspoon freshly ground pepper**
4 **(5-ounce) trout fillets**
¼ **cup sliced almonds, toasted**

1. Juice 2 lemons and thinly slice the third.

2. Bring ¼ cup of the lemon juice, 4 lemon slices, the wine, parsley, salt, and pepper to a boil in a nonstick skillet. Add the trout fillets, reduce the heat, and cover. Poach at a gentle boil until the fillets are just opaque in the center, about 5 minutes. Transfer the fillets to plates and spoon the poaching liquid over the fillets. Discard the lemon slices from the skillet. Top the trout with the remaining lemon slices and sprinkle with the almonds.

Per serving: 270 Cal, 11 g Fat, 1 g Sat Fat, 81 mg Chol, 623 mg Sod, 4 g Carb, 2 g Fib, 33 g Prot, 156 mg Calc. *POINTS: 6.*

Lemon Tips

- Look for firm, thin-skinned lemons, which have the most juice.
- Before squeezing a lemon, make sure it is at room temperature. Then roll on a hard surface, pressing firmly to loosen the juice.
- After you've squeezed a lemon, toss the rinds in the dish water to help cut grease and add sparkle.
- One medium lemon yields two to three tablespoons of juice and two to three teaspoons of zest.

Rainbow Trout in Orange Sauce

MAKES 4 SERVINGS

Although rainbow trout used to be a highly seasonal commodity, it is now farm-raised and readily available fresh—usually boned and butterflied—year-round. For a pretty garnish, simmer large strips of orange zest until they're pliable, about 15 minutes (simmering removes the bitterness); cut into thin strips and sprinkle over the fish.

1¼ **cups fresh orange juice**
  2 **tablespoons + ¼ cup all-purpose flour**
  1 **tablespoon unsalted butter**
 ¼ **cup chopped onion**
  4 **(6-ounce) rainbow trout fillets**

1. Whisk together the orange juice and 2 tablespoons of the flour in a small bowl.
2. Heat a small saucepan over medium heat. Add the butter and onion and cook, stirring occasionally, until the onion is translucent. Add the orange juice mixture and cook, stirring occasionally, until the sauce thickens and turns creamy, 8–10 minutes.
3. Meanwhile, heat a nonstick skillet. Dredge the fillets in the remaining ¼ cup of flour, then spray the fillets with nonstick spray. Put in the skillet and cook until browned on the outside and just opaque in the center, 2–3 minutes on each side. Spoon the sauce onto 4 plates and top each with a fillet.

Per serving: 342 Cal, 12 g Fat, 4 g Sat Fat, 108 mg Chol, 61 mg Sod, 18 g Carb, 1 g Fib, 37 g Prot, 127 mg Calc. ***POINTS: 8.***

shopping flash

Fresh orange juice is preferable for this sauce, but feel free to use a high-quality prepared juice. Don't use one from concentrate. If you're yearning for other citrus flavors, substitute the juice of three or four blood oranges or one large ruby red grapefruit for the orange juice.

Asparagus Frittata

MAKES 4 SERVINGS

For an extra-pretty touch to this already elegant dish, reserve some asparagus tips (leave them 3 to 4 inches long). Before you put the frittata in the oven, arrange them in a spoke pattern on top of the frittata.

24 **asparagus spears, cut into 2-inch lengths**
3 **large eggs**
6 **egg whites**
⅓ **cup grated Parmesan cheese**
¼ **cup fat-free milk**
2 **tablespoons minced chives**
¼ **teaspoon salt**
¼ **teaspoon freshly ground pepper**
4 **teaspoons olive oil**

1. Preheat the oven to 350°F.
2. Cook the asparagus in a pan of boiling water until barely tender, about 2 minutes. Drain and rinse with cold water, then drain again.
3. Whisk the eggs, egg whites, cheese, milk, chives, salt, and pepper in a bowl.
4. Heat the oil in an ovenproof nonstick skillet. Add the asparagus and sauté until coated with the oil. Reduce the heat to medium, pour in the eggs and stir quickly to combine. Cook until the eggs are set around the edges, about 5 minutes. Transfer the skillet to the oven and bake until the eggs are set, about 10 minutes.

Per serving: 218 Cal, 13 g Fat, 5 g Sat Fat, 172 mg Chol, 571 mg Sod, 6 g Carb, 1 g Fib, 20 g Prot, 281 mg Calc. *POINTS: 5.*

Braised Short Ribs

about last night
slow-cooker recipes

Braised Short Ribs

MAKES 6 SERVINGS

Since short ribs can be very high in fat, we brown the meat to render off a good amount of it. We like to serve this with a quick salad of boiled new potatoes, radish, and celery in a tangy vinaigrette.

1½ **pounds lean beef short ribs**
½ **cup flour**
1½ **teaspoons paprika**
 1 **teaspoon salt**
½ **teaspoon dry mustard**
 2 **onions, sliced and separated into rings**
 2 **garlic cloves, chopped**
 1 **cup light beer**

1. Heat a nonstick skillet over high heat. Brown the short ribs on all sides, then drain off all the fat. Sprinkle the ribs with the flour, paprika, salt, and mustard, then transfer to a slow cooker.
2. Stir in the onions, garlic, and beer, making sure the onions are under the ribs. Cook on High until the ribs are tender, about 3–4 hours.

Per serving: 295 Cal, 14 g Fat, 6 g Sat Fat, 72 mg Chol, 435 mg Sod, 12 g Carb, 1 g Fib, 26 g Prot, 23 mg Calc. *POINTS: 7.*

Cooking and Serving Slow-Cooker Fare

The recipes in this chapter include instructions for cooking at the High setting on a slow cooker. If you'll be away all day and want to prolong the cooking time, simply set on the Low setting and double the cooking time. Ready to eat? Think of a serving for most of these slow-cooker recipes as about 1 cup.

Marinara Sauce with Turkey Sausage

MAKES 8 SERVINGS

The secret to a good marinara sauce is patience for long, slow simmering, so a slow cooker provides the perfect medium. Serve over your favorite pasta.

2 **Italian-style turkey sausages, casings removed**
1 **onion, chopped**
1 **garlic clove, minced**
2 **(28-ounce) cans crushed tomatoes**
½ **teaspoon dried basil leaves, crumbled**
½ **teaspoon dried oregano leaves, crumbled**

1. Brown the sausage in a skillet, breaking it apart with a spoon. With a slotted spoon, transfer to a slow cooker. In the skillet, sauté the onion and garlic until softened. Add to the slow cooker, then stir in the tomatoes. Cover and cook on High until thickened, about 2 hours.
2. Stir in the basil and oregano; cook until the flavors are blended, about 1 hour longer.

Per serving: 50 Cal, 1 g Fat, 0 g Sat Fat, 5 mg Chol, 191 mg Sod, 9 g Carb, 2 g Fib, 3 g Prot, 42 mg Calc. *POINTS: 1.*

Teriyaki Chicken

MAKES 8 SERVINGS

Brown sugar and mustard combine to make a tangy, hot-sweet sauce in this easy classic. Serve over rice with an Asian-style cabbage slaw on the side.

1 (16-ounce) bag frozen broccoli, carrots, and water chestnuts
2 tablespoons quick-cooking tapioca
2 pounds skinless boneless chicken breasts, cubed
1 cup chicken broth
¼ cup packed brown sugar
¼ cup teriyaki sauce
2 tablespoons dry mustard
2 teaspoons grated orange zest
1 teaspoon ground ginger

1. Put the frozen vegetables in a slow cooker, then sprinkle with the tapioca. Put the chicken on top of the vegetables.

2. Mix the broth, brown sugar, teriyaki sauce, mustard, orange zest, and ginger in a bowl, stirring until the sugar dissolves. Pour over the chicken and cook on High until chicken is cooked through, 4–6 hours.

Per serving: 217 Cal, 4 g Fat, 1 g Sat Fat, 63 mg Chol, 443 mg Sod, 19 g Carb, 2 g Fib, 26 g Prot, 42 mg Calc. *POINTS: 4.*

Altering Recipes for a Slow Cooker

Want to make your favorite recipe do the slow-cook? Follow these simple guidelines to learn how.

• Liquids don't evaporate in a slow cooker, so decrease the amount of liquid by half—except in recipes that contain rice or barley, in which the amount of liquid stays the same.

• Dairy products like milk and sour cream should be added only during the last hour of cooking.

• Herbs added during the last hour of cooking will have a more pronounced flavor; those added with the other ingredients will blend in more.

• When thickening a sauce with flour or cornstarch at the end of cooking, increase the heat and cook for 15 to 25 minutes longer.

Use this chart as a guide to adjust the simmering time (not the total cooking time) of a recipe:

Dishes that simmer:	Cook in a slow cooker:	
15–30 minutes	1½–2½ hours on High	4–8 hours on Low
35–40 minutes	3–4 hours on High	6-10 hours on Low
50 minutes–3 hours	4–5 hours on High	8–18 hours on Low

Chicken and Bean Casserole

MAKES 6 SERVINGS

This is lovely with a salad or steamed cabbage. If you would rather use dried beans than canned, remember that they will need to be soaked overnight first.

2 (15-ounce) cans great Northern beans, rinsed and drained

1 cup water

2 ounces chorizo or turkey kielbasa, diced

1 large onion, chopped

1 carrot, sliced

4 garlic cloves, minced

2 (5- to 6-ounce) chicken thighs, skinned and cut into pieces

1 (14½-ounce) can stewed tomatoes

1 celery stalk, chopped

½ teaspoon dried marjoram

½ teaspoon freshly ground pepper

1 sage leaf, minced

1 bay leaf

⅛ teaspoon ground cloves

¼ cup chopped flat-leaf parsley

½ teaspoon salt

1. Put the rinsed beans and water into a slow cooker.

2. Heat a nonstick skillet over medium-high heat. Brown the sausage, then add the onion, carrot, and garlic and sauté until the garlic is golden. Transfer to the slow cooker, then add the chicken, tomatoes, celery, marjoram, pepper, sage, bay leaf, and cloves. Cook on High until the chicken is cooked through, 4–6 hours. Discard the bay leaf. Stir in the parsley and salt just before serving.

Per serving: 218 Cal, 5 g Fat, 2 g Sat Fat, 24 mg Chol, 53 mg Sod, 30 g Carb, 16 g Fib, 14 g Prot, 111 mg Calc. *POINTS: 4.*

Chicken Bonne Femme

MAKES 8 SERVINGS

Literally "Good Wife's Chicken," this homey, comforting French dish is delicious over rice or mashed potatoes.

3 **pounds chicken parts, skin removed**
2 **cups frozen baby onions**
1 **(16-ounce) bag baby carrots**
¾ **pound new potatoes, scrubbed
   and cut into 1-inch pieces**
1½ **cups low-sodium chicken broth**
2 **celery stalks, cut into 2-inch lengths**
2 **strips turkey bacon, diced**
1 **bay leaf**
¼ **teaspoon dried thyme leaves**
¼ **teaspoon freshly ground pepper**
¼ **cup chopped parsley**
2 **tablespoons chopped tarragon or mint**
1 **(2-inch) strip lemon zest**
2 **tablespoons fresh lemon juice**
½ **teaspoon salt**

1. Combine the chicken, onions, carrots, potatoes, broth, celery, bacon, bay leaf, thyme, and pepper in a slow cooker. Cover and cook on High until the chicken is cooked through, 4–6 hours. With a slotted spoon, transfer the chicken and vegetables to a platter. Cover with foil to keep warm.
2. Skim off any fat that has risen to the surface of the liquid remaining in the slow cooker. Discard the bay leaf. Stir in the parsley, tarragon, lemon zest, lemon juice, and salt; then spoon the sauce over the chicken and vegetables.

Per serving: 185 Cal, 5 g Fat, 1 g Sat Fat, 53 mg Chol, 280 mg Sod, 15 g Carb, 2 g Fib, 19 g Prot, 52 mg Calc. ***POINTS: 4.***

White Chili

MAKES 8 SERVINGS

If you crave chili but want something a little lighter in texture and flavor, try this variation which uses white beans and chicken.

4 cups low-sodium chicken broth
1 pound skinless boneless chicken breasts, cut into 1-inch pieces
2 (15-ounce) cans great Northern beans, rinsed and drained
2 medium zucchini, diced
2 onions, chopped
1 tablespoon ground cumin
2 garlic cloves, minced
1 teaspoon chili powder
1 cup frozen corn kernels
½ cup fat-free sour cream
½ teaspoon salt
Freshly ground pepper, to taste

1. Mix the broth, chicken, beans, zucchini, onions, cumin, garlic, and chili powder in a slow cooker. Cover and cook on High until the chicken is cooked through, about 3½ hours.

2. Stir in the corn and sour cream; cook until heated through, about 5 minutes longer. Season with the salt and pepper and serve.

Per serving: 193 Cal, 3 g Fat, 1 g Sat Fat, 34 mg Chol, 264 mg Sod, 19 g Carb, 6 g Fib, 21 g Prot, 64 mg Calc. *POINTS: 3.*

Beef Fajitas

MAKES 6 SERVINGS

This makes a great party dish. Serve the filling in your slow cooker's stoneware insert and let guests make their own fajitas. If you like, also set out bowls of chopped avocado and tomato, salsa, shredded lettuce, and fat-free sour cream.

1 **pound flank steak, trimmed and cut into 6 pieces**
1 **(14½-ounce) can Mexican-styled stewed tomatoes, drained**
1 **sweet onion, sliced**
1 **red bell pepper, seeded and sliced**
1 **green bell pepper, seeded and sliced**
¼ **cup canned diced jalapeño peppers**
2 **garlic cloves, minced**
1 **teaspoon chili powder**
1 **teaspoon ground cumin**
1 **teaspoon ground coriander**
¼ **teaspoon salt**
6 **(10-inch) flour tortillas**
⅓ **cup shredded reduced-fat taco cheese blend**

1. Mix the beef, tomatoes, onion, bell peppers, jalapeños, garlic, chili powder, cumin, coriander, and salt in a slow cooker. Cover and cook on High until the beef is tender, 4–5 hours.

2. Transfer the meat to a cutting board and cool slightly. Shred and return to the tomato sauce.

3. Just before serving, heat the tortillas according to package directions. Sprinkle the cheese along the center of the tortillas, then top with the beef mixture and fold.

Per serving: 313 Cal, 9 g Fat, 3 g Sat Fat, 36 mg Chol, 543 mg Sod, 30 g Carb, 4 g Fib, 27 g Prot, 143 mg Calc. **POINTS: 6.**

Beef Stew

MAKES 8 SERVINGS

Lean cuts of beef tend to be tougher than higher-fat cuts. Slow cooking is the perfect way to cook leaner beef—the steam created in the stoneware insert helps to tenderize the meat and retain its flavor.

1½ **pounds boneless beef bottom round, cubed**
 3 **tablespoons all-purpose flour**
 1 **pound small new potatoes, quartered**
 1 **(16-ounce) bag baby carrots**
 1 **(14½-ounce) can diced tomatoes**
½ **cup dry red wine**
 1 **onion, chopped**
 2 **garlic cloves, crushed**
 1 **teaspoon dried thyme leaves, crumbled**
 1 **tablespoon balsamic vinegar**
½ **teaspoon salt**

1. Mix the beef and flour in a large zip-close plastic bag; seal the bag and shake to coat the meat.

2. Mix the beef and flour, the potatoes, carrots, tomatoes, wine, onion, garlic, and thyme in a slow cooker. Cover and cook on High until the beef is tender, 5–6 hours. Stir in the vinegar and salt.

Per serving: 213 Cal, 4 g Fat, 1 g Sat Fat, 48 mg Chol, 137 mg Sod, 22 g Carb, 2 g Fib, 18 g Prot, 48 mg Calc. *POINTS: 4.*

cooking flash

Since the colors of food lose their vibrancy in a slow cooker, use garnishes to perk things up visually: chopped fresh parsley, cilantro, watercress, basil or other fresh herbs; chopped tomatoes, scallions, or red peppers; shredded carrots or cheese; nonfat yogurt or sour cream.

Sauerbraten

MAKES 8 SERVINGS

The longer you let this savory German specialty marinate, the sharper its flavor will be. Serve it over boiled potatoes, spaetzle, or no-yolk egg noodles.

1 cup red-wine or cider vinegar
2 onions, sliced
2 teaspoons caraway seeds
2 garlic cloves, crushed
2 bay leaves
½ teaspoon freshly ground pepper
1 (1½-pound) boneless rump roast, tied
1 carrot, sliced
1 parsnip, peeled and diced
½ cup low-sodium beef broth
3 gingersnap cookies, crumbled

1. Bring the vinegar, onions, caraway seeds, garlic, bay leaves, and pepper to a boil in a small saucepan. Let cool, then pour into a large zip-close plastic bag; add the beef. Seal the bag, squeezing out the air; turn to coat the beef. Refrigerate 1–3 days, turning the bag about every 8 hours.

2. Mix the beef and marinade with the carrot, parsnip, and broth in a slow cooker. Cover and cook on High until the beef is tender, 4–5 hours. With a slotted spoon, transfer the beef and all but ½ cup of the vegetables to a platter. Cover loosely with foil and let stand while you make the sauce.

3. Skim off and discard any fat that has risen to the surface of the cooking liquid. Discard the bay leaves. Transfer the remaining ½ cup of vegetables and the cooking liquid to a food processor or blender; add the gingersnaps and puree. If the sauce is too cool, pour into a medium saucepan and heat to serving temperature. Pour over the beef and vegetables.

Per serving: 181 Cal, 6 g Fat, 2 g Sat Fat, 47 mg Chol, 69 mg Sod, 9 g Carb, 2 g Fib, 20 g Prot, 29 mg Calc.
POINTS: 4.

Classic Beef Chili

MAKES 8 SERVINGS

To vary the different heat levels in chili, add different chile peppers to suit your tolerance. Habaneros are the hottest; Scotch bonnets pack a little less heat and have undertones of fruit and smoke; serranos have a biting heat and some acidity; while jalapeños have a vegetable flavor and, in this group at least, can be considered mild.

1 **pound lean ground beef
   (10% or less fat)**
2 **garlic cloves, finely chopped**
2 **tablespoons chili powder**
1 **teaspoon ground cumin**
1 **(28-ounce) can crushed tomatoes**
1 **(15-ounce) can red kidney beans,
   rinsed and drained**
1 **sweet onion, chopped**
¼ **cup canned diced chiles**
2 **tablespoons tomato paste**
Oregano sprigs

1. Cook the ground beef and garlic in a nonstick skillet, breaking apart the meat with a spoon, until browned. Drain off any fat. Add the chili powder and cumin and stir to coat the beef.

2. Mix the tomatoes, beans, onion, chiles, and tomato paste in a slow cooker. Stir in the beef mixture. Cover and cook on High until the flavors are blended, 4–5 hours. Garnish with oregano and serve.

Per serving: 142 Cal, 5 g Fat, 2 g Sat Fat, 35 mg Chol, 166 mg Sod, 10 g Carb, 4 g Fib, 14 g Prot, 43 mg Calc.
POINTS: 2.

Classic Beef Chili

Beef Stroganoff

MAKES 4 SERVINGS

Stroganoff gets its name from a nineteenth-century Russian diplomat, Count Paul Stroganov. This dish sometimes includes mushrooms; if you like, toss in a tablespoon or two of dried porcinis (no need to reconstitute beforehand). Serve over rice or no-yolk egg noodles.

1 pound boneless beef top round, cubed
1 cup beef broth
⅓ cup dry sherry
1 small onion, chopped
2 garlic cloves, minced
½ teaspoon dried oregano
¼ teaspoon salt
¼ teaspoon freshly ground pepper
⅛ teaspoon dried thyme
1 bay leaf
½ cup fat-free sour cream
¼ cup all-purpose flour
2 tablespoons water

1. Mix the beef, broth, sherry, onion, garlic, oregano, salt, pepper, thyme, and bay leaf in a slow cooker. Cover and cook on High until the beef is tender, 4–5 hours.
2. Mix the sour cream, flour, and water in a bowl. Stir about 1 cup of the hot liquid into the sour cream mixture, then stir the sour cream mixture into the stroganoff. Cover and cook until thick and bubbling, about 30 minutes. Discard the bay leaf before serving.

Per serving: 251 Cal, 5 g Fat, 2 g Sat Fat, 72 mg Chol, 405 mg Sod, 13 g Carb, 1 g Fib, 32 g Prot, 44 mg Calc.
POINTS: 5.

Veal Stew

MAKES 4 SERVINGS

Flavors tend to mellow in a slow cooker, so we stir in the mustard paste just before serving to give the stew a piquant bite.

STEW

- 3 cups shiitake mushrooms, sliced
- 10 ounces veal stew meat, trimmed and cubed
- 3 onions, sliced
- 1 cup baby carrots
- 1 cup canned diced tomatoes, drained
- ½ cup low-sodium beef broth
- ½ cup dry white wine
- 2 slices bacon, diced
- 2 bay leaves
- ½ teaspoon dried rosemary leaves, crumbled
- ½ teaspoon dried thyme
- ½ teaspoon dried marjoram
- ½ teaspoon freshly ground pepper

MUSTARD PASTE

- ⅓ cup finely chopped parsley
- 1 tablespoon capers, rinsed and finely chopped
- 1 tablespoon Dijon mustard
- 1 garlic clove, minced

1. Mix the stew ingredients in a slow cooker. Cover and cook on High until the veal is tender, 4–5 hours.

2. Mix the mustard paste ingredients in a small bowl. Cover and refrigerate until ready to use, up to 2 days.

3. Just before serving, stir the paste into the stew. Discard the bay leaves before serving.

Per serving: 260 Cal, 6 g Fat, 2 g Sat Fat, 65 mg Chol, 320 mg Sod, 27 g Carb, 5 g Fib, 22 g Prot, 85 mg Calc. **POINTS: 5.**

Mexican Lamb and Lentil Stew

MAKES 4 SERVINGS

This rich, soupy stew has complex flavor. Chipotles are dried, smoked jalapeño peppers; en adobo refers to the spicy sauce they're packed in. Look for them in cans in the Mexican food section of larger supermarkets or in Hispanic markets.

1 cup lentils, picked over, rinsed, and drained
1½ cups boiling water
1½ pounds plum tomatoes
2 large garlic cloves, unpeeled
1 teaspoon olive oil
2 onions, chopped
½ pound boneless lamb shoulder, trimmed and cubed
½ cup low-sodium beef broth
1 tablespoon pureed chipotles en adobo
½ teaspoon dried thyme
½ teaspoon dried oregano
¼ teaspoon cinnamon
2 bay leaves

1. Combine the lentils and boiling water in the slow cooker.

2. Set the broiler rack 4 inches from the heat. Preheat the broiler. Cover a baking sheet with foil. Set the tomatoes and garlic on the baking sheet and broil, turning often, until the tomatoes are charred and the garlic peel is deep brown, about 10 minutes. Cool slightly, then peel the tomatoes and garlic and put them in a food processor.

3. Meanwhile, heat the oil in a nonstick skillet. Add the onions and sauté until golden, then transfer half the onions to the food processor and the rest to the slow cooker. Add the lamb to the slow cooker.

4. Puree the vegetables, then stir them into the slow cooker. Add the broth, chipotles, thyme, oregano, cinnamon, and bay leaves. Cook on High until the lamb cubes are tender, 4–6 hours. Discard the bay leaves before serving.

Per serving: 321 Cal, 7 g Fat, 2 g Sat Fat, 40 mg Chol, 94 mg Sod, 41 g Carb, 8 g Fib, 26 g Prot, 75 mg Calc. ***POINTS: 5.***

Jambalaya

MAKES 6 SERVINGS

This Creole classic is traditionally simmered for a long time, so it's a natural for the slow cooker. It gets its name from the French word jambon, which means ham.

1 cup diced lean boiled ham
2 onions, coarsely chopped
2 celery stalks, sliced
½ green bell pepper, seeded and chopped
1 (28-ounce) can whole tomatoes
¼ cup tomato paste
3 garlic cloves, minced
1 tablespoon chopped parsley
½ teaspoon dried thyme
2 whole cloves
1 tablespoon vegetable oil
1 cup long-grain white rice
1 pound medium shrimp, peeled and deveined

1. Combine the ham, onions, celery, bell pepper, tomatoes, tomato paste, garlic, parsley, thyme, cloves, oil, and rice in a slow cooker. Cook on High 4–5 hours.
2. Add the shrimp and cook until the shrimp are pink, about 1 hour longer.

Per serving: 296 Cal, 5 g Fat, 1 g Sat Fat, 125 mg Chol, 513 mg Sod, 38 g Carb, 3 g Fib, 24 g Prot, 108 mg Calc. **POINTS: 6.**

Split Pea Soup

MAKES 8 SERVINGS

A warm bowl of hearty, long-simmered soup on a cold winter's evening—ahhh!

4 **cups water**
3 **carrots, peeled and thinly sliced**
1 **(16-ounce) bag dried green split peas,**
   picked over, rinsed and drained
3 **celery stalks, sliced**
1 **cup low-sodium chicken broth**
3 **slices Canadian bacon, diced**
1 **teaspoon salt**

Mix all the ingredients in a slow cooker. Cover and cook on High until vegetables and peas are tender, about 5 hours.

Per serving: 147 Cal, 1 g Fat, 0 g Sat Fat, 5 mg Chol, 431 mg Sod, 24 g Carb, 5 g Fib, 11 g Prot, 30 mg Calc. *POINTS: 2.*

Beans, Peas, Lentils, and Slow Cookers

Use this chart to make your own ready-to-use beans and skip the loads of sodium in canned beans.

Black beans	Full-flavored, perfect in soups and stews	Cook 1 pound dried beans in 7 cups water about 8½ hours on Low
Black-eyed peas	Earthy flavor; used in the classic dish Hoppin' John	Cook 1 pound dried peas in 6 cups water about 6½ hours on Low
Red kidney beans	Meaty flavor, mealy; good in chilis, red beans and rice	Cook 1 pound dried beans in 8 cups water about 10 hours on Low
Split peas	Creamy texture; great in hearty soups (especially those made with ham)	Cook 1 pound dried peas in 6 cups water about 6 hours on Low
White kidney beans	Richly flavored, creamy; good in soups and salads	Cook 1 pound dried beans in 6 cups water about 6½ hours on Low
Lentils	Brown, green, and red; common in ethnic dishes and purees	Cook 1 pound dried lentils in 6 cups water about 4 hours on Low
Chickpeas	Nutty taste, firm; used in falafel and hummus	Cook 1 pound dried chickpeas in 8 cups water about 10 hours on Low

Vegetable Curry Stew

MAKES 8 SERVINGS

Serve this dish over basmati rice or with warmed sesame pitas. We like to use barley to thicken the stew, but brown rice works well, too.

4 **carrots, chopped**
1 **(15-ounce) can chickpeas,
 rinsed and drained**
½ **pound green beans, trimmed
 and cut into 1-inch lengths**
2 **small all-purpose potatoes,
 peeled and chopped**
2 **onions, coarsely chopped**
2 **tablespoons pearl barley**
2 **teaspoons curry powder**
2 **garlic cloves, minced**
1 **teaspoon ground coriander**
¼ **teaspoon salt**
⅛ **teaspoon cinnamon**
1¾ **cups vegetable or chicken broth**
1 **(14½-ounce) can diced tomatoes**

1. Mix the carrots, chickpeas, green beans, potatoes, onions, barley, curry, garlic, coriander, salt, and cinnamon in a slow cooker. Add the broth. Cover and cook on High until the vegetables are tender, 4–5 hours.
2. Turn the slow cooker off and stir in the tomatoes; let stand, covered, 5 minutes.

Per serving: 124 Cal, 1 g Fat, 0 g Sat Fat, 0 mg Chol, 413 mg Sod, 22 g Carb, 6 g Fib, 6 g Prot, 63 mg Calc. *POINTS: 1.*

shopping flash

If green beans aren't in season, feel free to use a 10-ounce box of frozen cut green beans (no need to thaw them before using).

bonus!
ten in fifteen
best ever 15-minute recipes

Southwestern Frittata

Southwestern Frittata

MAKES 2 SERVINGS

This zesty egg creation makes a quick but quality dinner for two. Serve it with fresh fruit and mini-muffins or rolls. Note: If you'd rather not separate eggs, use ¼ cup fat-free egg substitute for the egg whites.

1 teaspoon olive oil

2 eggs

2 egg whites

¼ teaspoon salt

¼ teaspoon freshly ground pepper

½ onion, chopped

¼ red bell pepper, seeded and sliced

¼ green bell pepper, seeded and sliced

¼ cup shredded reduced-fat cheddar cheese

2 tablespoons salsa

In a medium nonstick skillet, heat the oil. In a small bowl, beat the eggs, egg whites, salt, and pepper until frothy. Sauté the onion and bell peppers until softened, about 5 minutes. Slowly pour in the egg mixture; sprinkle with the cheese. Cook, stirring gently, until slightly firm, 3–5 minutes. Slide the frittata onto a plate and turn over; slide back into pan to finish cooking, 1–2 minutes longer. Cut the frittata in half and roll up burrito-style. Serve topped with the salsa.

Per serving: 165 Cal, 9 g Fat, 3 g Sat Fat, 195 mg Chol, 455 mg Sod, 6 g Carb, 1 g Fib, 15 g Prot, 171 mg Calc. **POINTS: 4.**

shopping flash

For an easy fruit salad, pick up a few containers of cantaloupe and seedless watermelon chunks, as well as some fresh mint, when you're in the produce department. Add a squeeze of fresh lime juice to perk up the flavors.

Chicken Curry

MAKES 4 SERVINGS

Exotic flavorings like curry powder and mango chutney add pizzazz to basic chicken breasts. For extra sweetness, stir in a handful of golden raisins when you add the orange juice and broth. Serve over quick-cooking rice with green peas.

1 tablespoon vegetable oil
2 tablespoons all-purpose flour
1 tablespoon curry powder
1 teaspoon ground cumin
¼ teaspoon salt
4 (3-ounce) thin-sliced skinless chicken breasts (¼-inch thick)
½ cup orange juice
½ cup low-sodium chicken broth or water
2 tablespoons mango chutney
¼ cup fat-free sour cream
2 tablespoons chopped cilantro (optional)

1. In a large nonstick skillet, heat the oil. In a large sealable plastic bag, mix the flour, curry powder, cumin, and salt. Add the chicken and shake to coat.

2. Transfer the chicken to the skillet, shaking off any excess flour (reserve the remaining flour); sauté until cooked through, about 3 minutes on each side. Transfer the chicken to a platter and keep warm.

3. Stir the excess flour into the skillet, mixing with the pan juices. Gradually add the orange juice and broth, stirring constantly and scraping up the browned bits from the bottom of the skillet; stir in the chutney. Bring to a boil and cook, stirring constantly, until the mixture thickens, about 1 minute. Stir in the sour cream until blended; simmer 30 seconds. Spoon the sauce over the chicken and sprinkle with the cilantro (if using).

Per serving: 197 Cal, 6 g Fat, 1 g Sat Fat, 51 mg Chol, 293 mg Sod, 14 g Carb, 1 g Fib, 22 g Prot, 48 mg Calc. *POINTS: 4.*

shopping flash

If you can't find mango chutney, any fruit chutney will do. Or use an equal amount of peach jam or pineapple or ginger preserves.

Jerk Turkey Cutlets

MAKES 4 SERVINGS

Jerk is a seasoning that originated in the Caribbean, where it is used primarily on grilled chicken and pork. Since jerk seasoning is basically a mixture of hot and sweet spices and herbs, it's impossible to find a definitive recipe: As with curry powder in India, what goes into the blend is strictly up to the cook. These cutlets go great with yellow rice and a side salad made from jicama.

2 tablespoons red-wine vinegar
2 scallions, coarsely chopped
1 tablespoon packed light brown sugar
1 tablespoon fresh lime juice
2 garlic cloves, minced
1 teaspoon ground allspice
1 teaspoon ground ginger
½ teaspoon cinnamon
¼ teaspoon freshly ground pepper
⅛ teaspoon cayenne pepper
2 teaspoons vegetable oil
¾ pound thin-sliced skinless
   turkey breasts (¼-inch thick),
   halved crosswise

1. In a food processor or blender, puree the vinegar, scallions, brown sugar, lime juice, garlic, allspice, ginger, cinnamon, ground pepper, and cayenne.
2. In a large nonstick skillet, heat the oil. Sauté the turkey until golden brown, about 2 minutes. Stir in the seasoning mixture and turn the turkey over; sauté until the turkey is cooked through and coated with the seasoning, about 3 minutes.

Per serving: 175 Cal, 8 g Fat, 2 g Sat Fat, 55 mg Chol, 54 mg Sod, 5 g Carb, 1 g Fib, 19 g Prot, 27 mg Calc.
POINTS: 4.

cooking flash

If you like your food extra-spicy, throw in a seeded chopped jalapeño pepper and increase the cayenne to ¼ teaspoon. To make yellow rice, simply stir a pinch of turmeric into the cooking water, or use a pinch of saffron threads dissolved in 2 tablespoons boiling water.

Pork Medallions in Lemon-Thyme Sauce

MAKES 4 SERVINGS

The mixture of thickener (cornstarch here, but sometimes flour or arrowroot) and liquid is called a slurry; it's used to thicken sauces and gravies. To avoid lumps, always add the thickener to the liquid—don't pour the liquid over the thickener.

2 teaspoons olive oil

¾ pound pork tenderloin, cut into ¼-inch slices

1 teaspoon dried thyme leaves, crumbled

¼ teaspoon salt

¼ teaspoon freshly ground pepper

1 cup chicken broth

1 tablespoon cornstarch

Juice of 1 lemon (2–3 tablespoons)

1. In a large nonstick skillet, heat the oil. Add the pork in a single layer and sprinkle with the thyme, salt, and pepper. Sauté 2 minutes, then turn over and sauté until cooked through, 2–3 minutes.

2. Put the broth in a small bowl, then add the cornstarch and stir until smooth. Pour the broth mixture into the skillet with the lemon juice; simmer until slightly thickened and heated through, about 1 minute.

Per serving: 156 Cal, 8 g Fat, 2 g Sat Fat, 57 mg Chol, 437 mg Sod, 3 g Carb, 0 g Fib, 18 g Prot, 8 mg Calc.
POINTS: 4.

Veal Marsala

MAKES 6 SERVINGS

Thin-sliced cutlets, sometimes called scaloppine, are incredibly tender and lean. However, they can toughen quickly, so watch them carefully to prevent overcooking. Serve this with your favorite pasta.

½ **cup all-purpose flour**
¼ **teaspoon salt**
⅛ **teaspoon freshly ground pepper**
6 **(2½-ounce) thin-sliced veal cutlets (¼-inch thick)**
½ **teaspoon olive oil**
3½ **ounces shiitake mushrooms, cleaned, stemmed, and sliced**
⅔ **cup dry Marsala wine**
½ **cup chicken broth**

1. Mix the flour, salt, and pepper on a sheet of wax paper. Dredge the veal in the mixture to coat all over.

2. Heat the oil in a large nonstick skillet, then add the mushrooms. Sauté until they begin to soften, about 3 minutes. Spray each cutlet lightly with nonstick spray. Move the mushrooms to one side of the skillet, add the cutlets, and cook until lightly browned and cooked through, about 2 minutes on each side. Transfer the cutlets to a plate and keep warm.

3. Add the wine and broth to the skillet and cook until the alcohol has burned off and the sauce thickens and turns clear, about 3 minutes. Pour the sauce over the cutlets and serve.

Per serving: 163 Cal, 3 g Fat, 1 g Sat Fat, 57 mg Chol, 248 mg Sod, 11 g Carb, 1 g Fib, 15 g Prot, 16 mg Calc. *POINTS: 3.*

shopping flash

Thin-sliced chicken or turkey cutlets can be substituted for the veal if you prefer.

Texas Steaks with Veggie Salsa

MAKES 4 SERVINGS

Although this may seem like a labor-intensive way to prepare the zucchini, it results in a much prettier salsa. Save the insides to use in quick breads or muffins.

1 **medium zucchini**
2 **tomatoes, cored and finely diced**
1 **yellow bell pepper, seeded and finely diced**
1 **small red onion, diced**
¼ **cup chopped cilantro**
1 **tablespoon fresh lime juice**
1 **garlic clove, minced**
¾ **teaspoon salt**
¾ **teaspoon freshly ground pepper**
¼ **teaspoon chili powder**
¼ **teaspoon sugar**
4 **(4-ounce) filets mignons, trimmed and flattened ⅓-inch thick**

1. To make the salsa, trim the ends of the zucchini, then cut a ¼-inch slice down its length. Rotate so the zucchini is resting on the cut side and cut another ¼-inch slice; repeat on the remaining two sides. Dice the skin portions of the zucchini; reserve the inside for other use. Place in a medium bowl; add the tomatoes, bell pepper, onion, cilantro, lime juice, and garlic. Stir in ½ teaspoon of the salt and ½ teaspoon of the pepper.

2. To make the steaks, heat a cast-iron skillet or ridged grill pan over medium-high heat. In a small bowl, combine the chili powder and sugar with the remaining salt and pepper. Sprinkle the filets on both sides with the spice mixture. Cook the filets until done to taste, 1–2 minutes on each side for rare, 2 minutes on each side for medium-rare, 2½ minutes on each side for medium. Let stand 5 minutes, top with the salsa, and serve.

Per serving: 219 Cal, 9 g Fat, 4 g Sat Fat, 70 mg Chol, 508 mg Sod, 9 g Carb, 2 g Fib, 25 g Prot, 27 mg Calc. *POINTS: 5.*

Pan-Fried Flounder with Scallions, Corn, and Tomatoes

MAKES 4 SERVINGS

In summer, try to use fresh corn kernels scraped right from the cob in this colorful dish. Doing so will add a few minutes to the preparation time, but the sweet, buttery flavor makes it time well spent.

1 tablespoon olive oil
5 scallions, thinly sliced
2 cups fresh or thawed frozen corn kernels
1 pint cherry tomatoes, quartered
½ teaspoon salt
¼ teaspoon freshly ground pepper
4 (6-ounce) flounder fillets
1 tablespoon fresh lemon juice
1 tablespoon minced chives or flat-leaf parsley

1. In a large skillet, heat the oil. Sauté the scallions until softened, about 3 minutes. Add the corn, tomatoes, ¼ teaspoon of the salt, and ⅛ teaspoon of the pepper; cook until the tomatoes are softened, about 5 minutes. With a slotted spoon, transfer the vegetables to a platter and keep warm. **2.** Place the flounder fillets and lemon juice in the pan. Cook the flounder until it is just opaque in the center, 2–3 minutes on each side. Transfer the flounder to the platter with the vegetables; sprinkle with the remaining salt, pepper, and the chives. Serve at once.

Per serving: 279 Cal, 6 g Fat, 1 g Sat Fat, 82 mg Chol, 440 mg Sod, 22 g Carb, 4 g Fib, 35 g Prot, 52 mg Calc. ***POINTS: 5.***

shopping flash

When choosing flounder fillets, look for those that are pearly white in color, with a smooth surface without any gaps or breaks in the flesh. You can substitute any firm, white-fleshed fish (scrod, halibut, perch, or even catfish) for the flounder.

Salmon Croquettes

MAKES 6 SERVINGS

Believe it or not, canned salmon is higher in calcium than milk. (A 3½-ounce serving of canned salmon provides about 225 mg of calcium; 4 ounces of fat-free milk offers about 150 mg.) Just be sure to mash the soft bones instead of picking them out. If you happen to have leftover poached salmon on hand, by all means use it.

1 **tablespoon olive oil**
1 **(14¾-ounce) can pink salmon, drained**
1 **celery stalk, minced**
4 **scallions, thinly sliced**
1 **egg**
1 **tablespoon snipped dill**
½ **cup wheat germ**
4 **cups mixed salad greens**
½ **lemon, cut into wedges**

1. In a large nonstick skillet, heat the oil. Place the salmon in a medium bowl; pick out the skin, then mash the bones with a fork. Mix in the celery, scallions, egg, and dill; form into 12 log-shaped croquettes. Place the wheat germ on a sheet of wax paper; roll croquettes in the wheat germ.
2. Gently place the croquettes in the skillet; cook until lightly golden, 3–4 minutes on each side. Serve on the salad greens, with the lemon on the side.

Per serving: 165 Cal, 8 g Fat, 2 g Sat Fat, 74 mg Chol, 397 mg Sod, 5 g Carb, 1 g Fib, 17 g Prot, 157 mg Calc.
POINTS: 4.

cooking flash

For a spicy croquette accompaniment (and only an extra ½ ***POINT*** per 2 tablespoons), make a zesty mayo: Combine ½ cup fat-free mayonnaise with 1 tablespoon prepared horseradish; add a bit of dill and lemon zest for color and great flavor.

Salmon Croquettes

Salmon Teriyaki with Gingered Spinach

MAKES 2 SERVINGS

Teriyaki basting and glazing sauce is very thick, its consistency more like ketchup or barbecue sauce than the very thin, more common teriyaki sauce.

- **2 (5-ounce) salmon fillets, skinned**
- **1 teaspoon vegetable oil**
- **1 (10-ounce) bag triple-washed spinach, cleaned**
- **1 tablespoon reduced-sodium soy sauce**
- **½ teaspoon Asian (dark) sesame oil**
- **1 tablespoon grated peeled gingerroot**
- **2 tablespoons teriyaki basting and glazing sauce**

1. Spray a large, heavy nonstick skillet with nonstick cooking spray; heat. Cook the salmon until opaque in the center, 3–5 minutes on each side.

2. Meanwhile, in a large nonstick saucepan, heat the vegetable oil. Add the spinach, soy sauce, sesame oil, and gingerroot; cook, stirring constantly, until the spinach wilts, 3–5 minutes. Transfer the spinach to a platter; place the salmon over the spinach and brush with the teriyaki sauce.

Per serving: 268 Cal, 12 g Fat, 2 g Sat Fat, 76 mg Chol, 1,377 mg Sod, 9 g Carb, 4 g Fib, 33 g Prot, 163 mg Calc. **POINTS: 6.**

cooking flash

Like chicken, salmon has a very thin layer of fat under the skin. Leave the skin on while cooking (to help hold the fish together), but remove it before eating to reduce your fat intake.

Zesty Tofu

 MAKES 2 SERVINGS

Because soft or silken varieties will fall apart, be sure to use firm or extra-firm tofu in this vegetarian delight. Rice and broccoli florets make this a balanced Asian meal.

1 tablespoon reduced-sodium soy sauce
2 teaspoons honey
1 teaspoon white-wine vinegar
1 teaspoon vegetable oil
½ teaspoon minced peeled gingerroot
Pinch crushed red pepper flakes
1 cup firm or extra-firm tofu,
** cut into 1-inch cubes**
1 teaspoon dried bonito flakes,
** toasted (optional)**

1. In a large bowl, whisk the soy sauce, honey, vinegar, oil, gingerroot, and pepper flakes.
2. Divide the tofu between 2 bowls; pour the sauce over. Let stand 5 minutes. Sprinkle with the bonito flakes and serve.

Per serving: 115 Cal, 6 g Fat, 1 g Sat Fat, 0 mg Chol, 276 mg Sod, 10 g Total Carb, 0 g Fib, 6 g Prot, 40 mg Calc. **POINTS: 3.**

shopping flash

Bonito, sometimes called skipjack, is a member of the tuna family. Dried bonito flakes are commonly used in the Japanese broth called dashi; they impart a salty flavor and crunchy texture to the tofu. Look for bonito flakes in Asian groceries. Toasting them in a nonstick skillet or toaster oven will add a little crunch.

DRY AND LIQUID MEASUREMENT EQUIVALENTS

If you are converting the recipes in this book to metric measurements, use the following chart as a guide.

TEASPOONS	TABLESPOONS	CUPS	FLUID OUNCES
3 teaspoons	1 tablespoon		½ fluid ounce
6 teaspoons	2 tablespoons	⅛ cup	1 fluid ounce
8 teaspoons	2 tablespoons plus 2 teaspoons	⅙ cup	
12 teaspoons	4 tablespoons	¼ cup	2 fluid ounces
15 teaspoons	5 tablespoons	⅓ cup minus 1 teaspoon	
16 teaspoons	5 tablespoons plus 1 teaspoon	⅓ cup	
18 teaspoons	6 tablespoons	¼ cup plus 2 tablespoons	3 fluid ounces
24 teaspoons	8 tablespoons	½ cup	4 fluid ounces
30 teaspoons	10 tablespoons	½ cup plus 2 tablespoons	5 fluid ounces
32 teaspoons	10 tablespoons plus 2 teaspoons	⅔ cup	
36 teaspoons	12 tablespoons	¾ cup	6 fluid ounces
42 teaspoons	14 tablespoons	1 cup minus 2 tablespoons	7 fluid ounces
45 teaspoons	15 tablespoons	1 cup minus 1 tablespoon	
48 teaspoons	16 tablespoons	1 cup	8 fluid ounces

Note: Measurement of less than ⅛ teaspoon is considered a dash or a pinch.

VOLUME	
¼ teaspoon	1 milliliter
½ teaspoon	2 milliliters
1 teaspoon	5 milliliters
1 tablespoon	15 milliliters
2 tablespoons	30 milliliters
3 tablespoons	45 milliliters
¼ cup	60 milliliters
⅓ cup	75 milliliters
½ cup	125 milliliters
⅔ cup	150 milliliters
¾ cup	175 milliliters
1 cup	225 milliliters
1 quart	1 liter

OVEN TEMPERATURE	
250°F	120°C
275°F	140°C
300°F	150°C
325°F	160°C
350°F	180°C
375°F	190°C
400°F	200°C
425°F	220°C
450°F	230°C
475°F	250°C
500°F	260°C
525°F	270°C

WEIGHT	
1 ounce	30 grams
¼ pound	120 grams
½ pound	240 grams
¾ pound	360 grams
1 pound	480 grams

LENGTH	
1 inch	25 millimeters
1 inch	2.5 centimeters